Merry Christmas 94

Dad love

Susan

FRESH
IS BEST

VOGUE

COOKERY COLLECTION

FRESH
IS BEST

HAMLYN

First published in 1988 by
The Hamlyn Publishing Group
Michelin House, 81 Fulham Road
London SW3 6RB

ISBN 0 600 56004 X

Printed by Mandarin Offset in Hong Kong

Text and photographs supplied by Vogue Ausralia

Vogue Australia Editor-in-Chief **June McCallum**
Vogue Entertaining Guide Editor **Carolyn Lockhart**
Food Editor **Joan Campbell**

Publishers' acknowledgments
Artworks: Maggie Smith (borders), Paul Cooper
(15); *Editor:* Carolyn Pyrah; *Coordinator:* Nicola
Hill; *Contributing Editor:* Suzy Powling; *Art Editor:*
Pedro Prá-Lopez; *Designer:* Michelle Stamp/Crucial
Books; *UK Consultant:* Jenni Fleetwood; *Produc-
tion Controller:* Eleanor McCallum.

Vogue Australia would like to thank the following for their invaluable contribution:

Margie Agostini (Stuffed Artichokes and Anchovy Sauce 24); Chalie Amatykul, Thai Cooking School, The Oriental, Bangkok (Chicken Satays with Peanut Sauce 63, Panaeng Paste 63); Mark Armstrong, Pegrum's, Sydney (Cornet of Trout with Squash Flowers, Tomato and Chervil Beurre Blanc 32, Crab Salad with Truffle Mayonnaise 33, Scallop and Bean Salad with Truffle Mayonnaise 38, Feuilleté of Rabbit with Pea Purée and Sorrel Sauce 66, Beurre Blanc 67); Tara Barry (Veal Rolls with Lemon Mousse Sauce 72); Mogens Bay Esbensen (Lobster with Mint 46); Virginia Bevan (Muesli 10); Michel Beyls (La Soupe Froide de Melon à la Canelle 81, Strawberry Ice-cream 82, Fresh Mango Ice-cream 84); Tony Bilson, Bilsons, Sydney (Escalopes of Salmon with Sauce Poivrade 51); Andrew Birley, Anders Ousback Catering, Sydney (Salad of Seafood 'Cordon Rubis' 40, Lime Mayonnaise, 40); Andrew Blake, Chez Oz, Sydney (Poached Chicken on Leeks with a Pear and Ginger Confit 62-63, Beef Fillet Carpaccio wtih Saffron and Parmesan Slices 68, La Coupe Ninoshka 81); Lydia Bonnin (Stuffed Lettuce in Broth 71); Max and Diana Bowden (Rum Punch 92); Catherine Brandel, The Robert Mondavi Winery, California (Grilled Tuna Niçoise 58); Marieke Brugman, Howqua Dale Gourmet Retreat, Victoria (Mussel and Leek Tarts with Saffron Champagne Sauce 32, Fish Plait with Tomato Basil Sauce 50); Bridget Buckworth (Fish Fan 59); Joan Campbell (Tomato Soup with Fennel and Basil Bavarois 19, Parsnip and Green Pea Soup 19, Fennel Soup 21, Vegetable Medley with Hollandaise Sauce 21, Avocados with Prawn Mayonnaise 29, Bread Salad 36, Spaghetti Squash Salad 36, Salad of Tomatoes and Basil 36, Spring Toss of Prawns 46, Fillets of White Fish with Crab and Leek Sauce 50, Grilled Tuna Steaks with Basil Butter 54, Fresh Fish Steaks with Aromatic Vegetables and Herbs 54-55, Escalopes of Sea Trout with Lime Sabayon Sauce on a bed of Leek and Carrot Julienne 58-59, Boardroom Fillet 70, Béarnaise Sauce 70, Watermelon with Lemon Cheese 84, Raspberry Mascarpone Cream 84, Pine Nut Biscuits 84, Fresh Fruits with Hot Sabayon 85); Joan Campbell for THE AUSTRALIAN MEAT AND LIVESTOCK CORPORATION's promotions in Vogue Entertaining Guides (Tomato Soufflés 26, Côte de Beouf with Aïoli 69, Individual Rosti 70, Noisettes of Lamb served on Onion Soubise with Melting Mint Butter 74);

Robyn Clubb (Fish or Prawn Balls with Vegetables and Barbecued Pork 50); Serge Dansereau, The Regent, Sydney (Rack of Lamb Stuffed with Courgettes 75); Wayne Davis (Marinated Côte de Beouf 72-73); Greg Doyle, Pugliny's, Sydney (Feuilleté of French Mushrooms 21, Brandy Cornet of Berries 90); Peter Doyle (Salad of Squid, Prawns and Avocado 40); Steven Elliot (Tomatoes Varenne 29); Toni Ellis (Sinigang na Hipon 20); Jenny Ferguson (Lobster and Pear Salad 48); Tansy Good and Marc Bouten, Tansy's Restaurant, Melbourne (Lobster with Saffron Pistils 46); Margot Grace (Fillet Steak with Raisins, Served with Mushroom and Carrot Timbales 72, Deboned Loin of Lamb with Port Wine Sauce 75, Demi-Glace Sauce 75); Sue Gray (Oysters and Caviar 45); Pia Griffin (Sillisalaatti 56); Consuelo Guinness (Calamare Salad with Cucumber and Cumin 53); Gabrielle Haumesser (Truite aux Amandes 52); Christopher Hayes (Pochouse 55); Barbara Heine (Rare Fillet of Beef with Mustard Béarnaise Sauce 68); Judith Henderson (Vegetable and Chicken Terrine 28); François and Ingrid Henry (East-West Hors-d'Oeuvres 28); Iain Hewitson (Peach Melba Revisited 82); Chantal Irvine (John Dory à la Dugléré 54); Cath Kerry, Petaluma Restaurant, Bridgewater, SA (Prawn Custard 33, Poussins Filled with Spiced Black Rice 66); Jean Jacques Lale-Demoz, Jean Jacques by the Sea, Melbourne (Truite Farcie au Saumon Fumé 56); Lamrock Café, Sydney (Soda-licious 11); Richard Lovett, Burnham Beeches Country Estate, Victoria (Asparagus with Quail Egg Salad and Chive Vinaigrette 28-29, Strawberries and Cream in Crisp Pastry Punnets 89); Jean-Luc Lundy (Lobster with Vanilla Sauce 44); Lynch's, Melbourne (Calamare in Dill Vinaigrette with Tomato Salad 29); Sandy Lynch (Paillard of Lamb Vinaigrette 76); Robyn MacIntosh (Zuppa di Pesce 48); Patrick Mahieu, La Normandie, Sydney (Stuffed Loin of Pork with a Rosemary Crust 68-69); Michael Manners, Glenella, Blackheath, NSW (Scallop Quenelles with Prawn Sauce 44); The Mansion on Turtle Creek Hotel, Dallas, USA (Fresh Raspberry Frappé 92); Michael McCarty of Michael's Restaurant, Los Angeles, USA (Sorbet 80); Brian and Fay McGuigan (Vegetable Platter with Curry Mayonnaise 23, Courgette Soufflé 24, Swedish Potatoes 65, Honeyed Buttered Carrots 65, Broccoli with Lemon Butter 65, Chicken Fillets in Pink Peppercorn and Brandy Sauce 65); Paul Merrony (Strawberry Sablés 86); Michael Miller (Gado Gado 38, Bananas with Mango Coconut Sauce 85, Grapefruit Punch 94); Mount Lofty House, Crafers, SA (Lobster and Mango Salad with

Chilli Mint Dressing 38); John Normyle (Greek Lemon Soup 19); Julie O'Connor and Mary Ellis (Warm Salad of Quail with Lardons and Croûtons 39, Duck Breasts with Ginger 64-65); Anders Ousback (The Wharf Fougaffe 22, Orange and Ginger Salad 84, Poached Pears with Passionfruit Syrup 89); Elise Pascoe and John Kelly (Leek Pavé with Ginger Vinaigrette 23); Christian Raboisson (Individual Pear or Raspberry Tarts 86); Carole Roet (Goat's Cheese with Fresh Garden Herbs 90); Michel Roux, The Roux Brothers on Patisserie (Tomato Sorbet 26); Martin Seubert and Rudi Satz, The Casbah, Trinity Beach, Qld (Kotopoulo Avgolemono 62); Leigh Stone-Herbert, Gravetye Manor, United Kingdom (Poached Eggs on Artichoke Hearts with Mousseline Sauce 30, Poached Fillets of Dover Sole on Noodles with Lobster Medallions and Chive Butter 53); Michael Symons and Jennifer Hillier, The Uraidla Aristologist, Uraidla, SA (Orange Soufflés 86); Claudia Thomas (Chilled Tomato and Dill Soup 18); Mariella Totaro (Mussels with Fresh Pepper 31); Jeremiah Tower, Stars, San Francisco, USA (Cod Carpaccio with Coriander Vinaigrette, Caviar and Black Bean Cream 52); Jay and Julie Tulloch (Beouf à la Ficelle 70, Potatoes Janet 70); Maria Valmorbida (Fruit Cup 92); John Vanderveer (Trout and Prawn Timbales 30-31, Cantaloupe Mousseline with Rhubarb Ice-cream 81); Nicole Vanson (Roasted Goat's Cheese Salad 29); Penny Walker (Lamb Rib-Eye Fleur-de-lis 76); Francis Yin (Tamarind Prawns Wrapped in Lemon Grass 45).

Our thanks to the following for permission to reproduce these recipes:

Whelks in Garlic Butter copyright © Jean-Jacques Lale-Demoz from Jean Jacques Seafood, Thomas Nelson Australia.

Grateful thanks to the following photographers:

Michael Cook 27, 31, 34, 41, 57, 67, 83; **David Haddon** 49, 73; **John Hay** 39, 45, 64, 77, 78, 91, 93; **Peter Johnson** 18; **Geoff Lung** 52, 63, 85, 94; **George Seper** 2, 6, 8, 11, 14, 20, 25, 42, 59, 80, 87; **Rodney Weidland** 16, 22, 37, 47, 51, 55, 60, 69, 70, 71, 74, 88; *The Fresh Is Best Test Kitchen*, NSW Department of Agriculture 12, 13.

CONTENTS

INTRODUCTION

A magic touch for a fresh approach,
entertaining ideas that are best, naturally

Welcome to this special volume of the *Vogue Cookery Collection*, the series of cookbooks designed to help you make every meal one to remember. At *Vogue*, the policy is to endorse food which is fresh and at its seasonable best and this is what this book is all about: recipes which are nutritionally best for you.

All the recipes are as attractive to taste as they are to the eye and all are very suitable for entertaining, from weekend breakfasts to formal dinners. They have been collected from a variety of people around the world, some of them professional cooks, the others amateur in the best sense of the word – meaning they are true lovers of what they do. The need for balance and for moderation is stressed, so sauces for meat and fish dishes as well as desserts have a light texture, and main courses are frequently accompanied by side salads. Cream is used occasionally, but rich puddings are preferably made with eggs, because of their nutritional value. Similarly, ice-creams frequently give way to light and refreshing fruit-flavoured sorbets.

Presentation – always important – is enhanced by simple and fresh garnishes, such as mint, grown perhaps in a tub by the kitchen door, or wild strawberry leaves.

Notoriously rich food and food additives and preservatives have come under recent suspicion. In *Fresh Is Best* you will discover a wealth of ideas which are not only a pleasure to look at and a joy to taste, but which can also be regarded as wholesome because of their natural freshness.

Sun-ripened peppers in glorious abundance and fiery chillies fresh and ready for use summon up all that's best about the exotic vegetables of late summer, full of the season's goodness and as irresistible to sight and touch as they are succulent to eat

8

FRESH IS BEST

*Natural ingredients and fresh presentation,
the secrets of successful entertaining*

The standard which governed the selection of recipes for this new cookbook means that the ingredients also lend themselves to beautiful presentation. Guests will feel doubly welcome when they discover that their hosts have taken time and trouble to ensure that food looks as good as it undoubtedly tastes.

Each recipe has a common denominator in the imagination shown in making the most of fresh, seasonal ingredients. As far as possible we have avoided anything that is smoked, salted, dried or canned. Even delicious smoked fish is high in salt and therefore it is better in small quantities. So when it comes to preserving food or keeping ingredients fresh, use the most natural methods. Freezing is an obvious example because nothing is added and, if the food is correctly prepared and frozen, the texture and flavour is not altered in any way. Marinades tenderise, flavour and preserve in the short term with the use of natural citrus juices, fresh herbs and a judicious amount of oil.

Discover foods which freeze well and avoid freezing those that don't. Vegetables fall into the latter category when whole, but frozen vegetable soups and purées are a wonderful standby. Meat may be frozen, but seafood, with its delicate flavours, is best fresh.

Enjoy creating a pleasant, welcoming atmosphere in which guests can relax. Even the most formal summer dinner may be served out of doors. Clever use of lighting – candles or lamplight – and appropriate table linen and accessories create a glamorous setting to enhance beautifully prepared fresh and natural food.

Tradition has it that the finest way to eat asparagus is to cook it the moment it's picked, bundling the tender spears straight into the steamer. Nothing more than a squeeze of lemon and a hint of melted butter is needed to make the most of its unique flavour.

A FRESH START

Breakfast should be substantial enough to give energy at the outset of the day, yet light enough to allow a relaxed and positive approach. There is no need for a cooked breakfast if you know that there is a lunch or dinner appointment ahead of you with fish or meat on the menu.

A great start can be made each morning with fruit. Keep a supply of juices in the refrigerator, although it is better to squeeze your choice of fruit fresh each day. Mix fresh fruit pieces with natural yogurt and, if you enjoy cereal (see panel at right for a delicious muesli recipe) try it mixed with natural yogurt or freshly squeezed juice instead of milk.

Make the breakfast ritual as relaxed as possible. Try substituting herbal teas – mint is cleansing and reviving, rosehip fragrant and filled with vitamin C and lemon balm is soothing – for your usual brew of coffee or tea. Both contain the stimulant caffeine, and too much of this should be avoided. Because the rest of your day may include work or social situations in which coffee or tea will play a part, learn to substitute whenever possible.

Cereals should be free from salt and sugar. Never underestimate the nutritional benefits of oats, that most health-giving of all cereals. The Scots have a theory that a meal of fish (particularly herring) and oatmeal will provide all the nourishment and vitamins needed. This perfect balance is important in all meals, but particularly for a fresh start each day.

MUESLI

Makes 4 kg/8 lb

400 g/14 oz rolled oats
350 g/12 oz bran
225 g/8 oz wheatgerm
75 g/3 oz shredded coconut
100 g/4 oz crushed mixed nuts
100 g/4 oz ground hazelnuts
1 kg/2 lb plain mixed unsalted nuts
150 g/5 oz sesame seeds
75 g/3 oz pine nuts
150 g/5 oz sunflower seeds
575 g/1¼ lb honey
350 ml/12 fl oz oil
350 g/12 oz chopped dried fruit
   (sultanas, dried apricots, dried apple)

Mix together all the ingredients except the dried fruit and spread evenly on baking sheets. Place the sheets in a preheated 180°C/350°F, Gas Mark 4 oven and toast the mixture until it is golden brown. Keep turning it over as it toasts. Watch it carefully, as it will burn easily.

Just before the end of the cooking time, add the dried fruit. The fruit should dry out a little but not enough to toughen and become hard. Remove the mixture from the oven and spread it on paper towels on baking sheets. Let it become completely cold before putting it in airtight containers to store.

SODA-LICIOUS

Serves 6

2 oranges, peeled
1 kiwifruit, skin removed
½ medium honeydew melon,
    peeled and seeds removed
200 g/7 oz watermelon (after
    seeds and rind are removed)
pulp from 4 passionfruit
225 g/8 oz ripe strawberries, hulled
250 ml/8 fl oz orange juice
450 g/1 lb Greek yogurt
lemon juice

garnish:
6 slices pineapple, cut in quarters
3 passionfruit, halved
2 kiwifruit, cut in slices
slices of green apple
slices of orange
slices of peeled banana
slices of cantaloupe melon
slices of ogen melon
spikes from a pineapple top

TO PREPARE THE FRUIT: dice all the
fruit. Place in a serving bowl and
cover with orange juice mixed with a
little lemon juice. Serve with a large
helping of Greek yogurt. Garnish
with slices of fruit and serve
immediately.

*Greet mornings in the best possible way
with a beautifully served breakfast based
on fresh fruit*

FRESH INGREDIENTS

The freshest ingredients that immediately spring to mind are, of course, fruit and vegetables. If your garden is large enough, you may be able to grow your own supplies; whether you can or not, make a friend of the local greengrocer, or find a good farm shop or supermarket with daily deliveries of top quality produce, readily available at its best when in season. Always look for fruit and vegetables that are a good, bright colour, have no blemishes, are firm to the touch and which have a bloom of freshness.

Clean vegetables thoroughly so that not only is all dirt removed, but also any traces of pesticides. If possible, eat vegetables and fruit which have been organically grown.

The flavour of fresh ginger enhances many oriental recipes and combines well with sweet and savoury dishes

The general rule about peeling vegetables and fruit is: don't, unless absolutely essential. The most nutritious part is often just below the skin, especially in tomatoes, potatoes and apples. Prepare them as close as possible to cooking time to avoid a loss of nutrients.

Vegetables should be just cooked, firm to the bite and retaining their colour. A good yardstick for cooking them is to remember that vegetables grown below the ground – potatoes, parsnips, carrots, and so on – should have a cold water start; those grown above – beans and leafy vegetables – benefit from a boiling water start.

Steaming is regarded as the best method of cooking vegetables because it eliminates loss of minerals and vitamins into the water. Sautéing is a method which should be completed quickly, using a minimum of fat so that not too much is absorbed, as fat aggravates digestive problems.

Full of vitamins and flavour, sorrel is a delicious leaf vegetable in salads or lightly cooked, and makes a fine soup

Vegetables and herbs of the onion family have been an enduring dietary staple since ancient times and are easy to grow

Use a simple marinade, based on virgin olive oil and tangy lemons, and spice it with pepper to tenderise meat

Fruit in any form is always a welcome and refreshing finish. Apples and pears provide economical and appetising desserts, but it is in summer that fruits come into their own, providing the basis for countless puddings, or piled bountifully into large bowls. Consider some options: melons can be sliced, cut in crescent-shaped wedges or arranged in clusters of tiny balls; berry fruits served on their own, piled into attractive dishes, puréed for sauces or made into refreshing sorbets.

Meat and fish are the basis of most main course recipes and learning to recognise a good cut is an essential part of healthy meal planning. Discover the leading suppliers of both items in your area – be fussy; never be satisfied with second best.

Fish markets generally have the freshest fish of all – unless, of course, you can catch the fish yourself. Fish should be cooked as soon as possible after landing and, with its subtle flavour, needs only the simplest methods of cooking and the simplest sauces to enhance it. Poaching and steaming are the preferred ways to cook fish because these methods retain the flavour and texture better than any other. If you poach, reserve the nutritious liquid for making a sauce or fish stock. Sauces should be light – a hollandaise or a béarnaise, perhaps – and, to avoid rich ingredients, in some recipes try substituting natural yogurt for cream. Avoid frying fish and grill it instead, as quickly as possible, on a preheated grill. Diagonal cuts in the thickest part will hasten the process, and fish steaks or fillets will need brushing with a little more oil or melted butter than whole fish. Lemon juice enhances the flavour of fish and is a wonderful basis for dressings for cold fish and fish salads.

Over the past few years white meat such as chicken has been accounted more nutritious than red meat because of its lower fat content (provided that the skin has been removed). Red meat, properly trimmed, will give a substantial portion of daily vitamin and mineral requirements. Overcooking meat will remove most of the valuable vitamins; grill, rather than fry, meat and use its natural juices to make sauces and gravies. Trim off all excess fat before cooking, and don't add extra oils when roasting – the fat from the meat itself is sufficient.

Demi-glace is a basis for many classic sauces – a jellied stock which is always useful to have on hand in the freezer. Don't worry if you don't have calves' feet, veal bones or pigs' trotters to make it. Other meat bones, such as mutton, may be used, although they are not so gelatinous.

Nothing compares with the pleasures of succulent fruits like lychees, their crimson skins encasing sweet white flesh

Puddings and desserts are often grand and may be extremely rich and very elaborate. While no one would deny the pleasure of these splendid offerings at the end of the meal, they need not be over-rich. Additional sugar in any fruit pudding is often unnecessary; the natural sweetness of fruit should be sufficient. Instead of making a syrup for a fruit salad, try using a blend of freshly squeezed fruit juices. (Lemon juice will help prevent cut soft fruits from discolouring.) Serve cream separately so that guests may take as much or as little as they like and always offer cheese as a savoury alternative to a dessert.

Enhance drinks and desserts naturally with slivers of fruit and cucumber, sprigs of mint, borage leaves and edible flowers for a fresh colour contrast.

A platter of carefully arranged and colourful fruits is the perfect way to end a meal – or start the day!

POACHING AND STEAMING

When it comes to cooking, to make the most of fresh and natural ingredients two methods are preferred: poaching and steaming. The following specialist items of equipment are a sound investment for easy preparation.

BAMBOO STEAMER 1

Not just for Chinese cookery. Because steam doesn't collect on the inside of the lid, drops of water do not fall on delicate ingredients. Steamers come in various sizes in sets of two tiers with a lid.

EXPANDING WIRE BASKET 2

A simple addition for your *batterie de cuisine*. The basket fits over most saucepans, providing an extra steamer or double boiler.

DOUBLE BOILER 3

Essential for steaming vegetables. Simmering water in the lower section does not come into contact with vegetables in the upper part and they remain firm and retain natural colour.

ASPARAGUS KETTLE 4

An especially tall container to hold asparagus upright while cooking. The bundles of asparagus are placed in sufficient simmering salted water — to come within 2.5 cm/1 inch of the tips. Always cook asparagus tied in bundles to prevent the delicate heads from moving around and breaking.

FISH KETTLE 5

The best way to cook a whole fish as well as steaks and fillets. The rack holding the fish is placed over boiling water, and the fish remains firm and full of flavour.

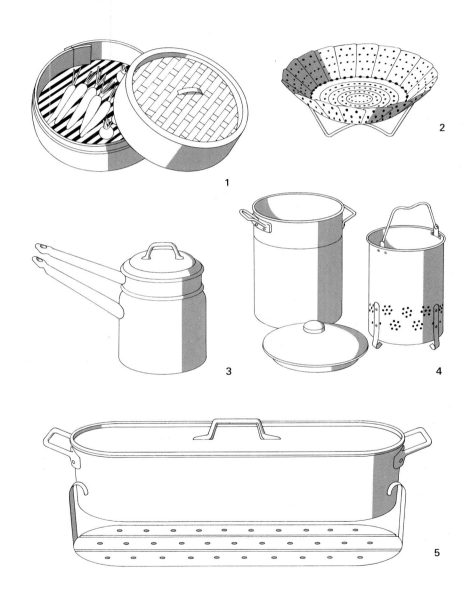

SOUPS & STARTERS

First impressions: a collection of recipe ideas that are naturally fresh and flavourful

The first course, often considered the simplest of all, is frequently the one which offers the greatest challenge. Not only must it be visually appealing and stimulate the appetite for following courses, but it must also offer a contrast while being complementary to them.

In this regard, food that is fresh and natural is an excellent choice – as well as a nutritious one. The first chapter embraces three categories: soups, vegetable and fish starters. Soups include a wide range of light options. Chilled Tomato and Dill (perfect for summer entertaining), flavourful Parsnip and Green Pea and the exotic Sinigang na Hipon (sour prawn soup) from the Philippines.

Vegetables provide the basis of a host of colourful first courses. Try a simple platter of vegetables, such as celery, mushrooms and artichoke hearts served with a curry mayonnaise; a refreshing Tomato Sorbet to cleanse the palate; or a delicately coloured Courgette Soufflé, which has the added advantage that it doesn't sink as soon as it is removed from the oven.

Fresh fish can be used in many ways: mussels in tiny tartlets with leeks and a saffron champagne sauce are easy to serve and just right to eat with pre-dinner drinks if required. More elaborate, and almost irresistible, is a cornet of trout fillet, filled with a prawn mousse and garnished with squash flowers. Whatever your choice, remember that freshly-picked garnishes – herbs, flowers and baby vegetables – will give natural appeal.

The first course offers an ideal opportunity to serve as a featured item delicate and tender mushrooms. Feuilleté of French Mushrooms (see page 21) sets off the flavour of cèpes, chanterelles and morels with an aromatic sauce and a contrasting lid of golden puff pastry

SOUPS

CHILLED TOMATO AND DILL SOUP

Chilled soups are perfect for outdoor entertaining in summer.

SERVES 6

4 large ripe tomatoes, skinned and sliced
1 medium onion, sliced
1 clove garlic
1 teaspoon salt
¼ teaspoon freshly ground black pepper
2 tablespoons tomato purée
¼ teaspoon Tabasco
4 tablespoons water
2 sprigs dill
50 g/2 oz cooked macaroni
250 ml/8 fl oz chicken stock
175 ml/6 fl oz single cream

GARNISH:
soured cream
2 sprigs fresh dill, chopped

Place the sliced tomatoes in a saucepan with the onion, garlic, salt, pepper, tomato purée, Tabasco, water and dill. Cover and cook slowly until the tomatoes and onions are soft.

Place the mixture in a blender or food processor with the cooked pasta, stock and cream, and process until smooth. Transfer to a bowl and leave in the refrigerator for 1-2 hours to chill. Garnish with soured cream and chopped dill.

Chilled Tomato and Dill Soup is cool but rich in texture and nourishing

TOMATO SOUP WITH FENNEL AND BASIL BAVAROIS

SERVES 6

FENNEL AND BASIL BAVAROIS:
2 large fennel bulbs
salt
lemon juice
20 basil leaves
2 teaspoons gelatine
freshly ground pepper
150 ml/¼ pint whipping cream, whipped

TOMATO SOUP:
8 large, ripe red tomatoes, cored and
  chopped roughly
pinch of sugar
1 teaspoon grated lemon rind
lemon juice to taste
salt
freshly ground pepper

TO MAKE THE FENNEL AND BASIL BAVAROIS: cut the fennel bulbs in pieces and cook them in boiling salted water with the lemon juice until they are tender. Drain well. Place the fennel in a blender or food processor and work to a purée. Add the basil leaves and purée the mixture again.

Dissolve the gelatine in a little warm water and add it to the blender. Purée again. Transfer the mixture to a bowl, season with salt and pepper to taste and fold in the cream. Place the mixture in a glass bowl, cover it and leave in the refrigerator to set.
TO MAKE THE TOMATO SOUP: purée the tomatoes in a blender. Add the sugar, lemon rind, lemon juice and salt and pepper to taste. Purée until the texture is smooth. Press the purée through a strainer into a clean bowl and chill in the refrigerator.
TO SERVE: pour the soup into six large soup bowls and place a spoonful of bavarois in the centre of each.

PARSNIP AND GREEN PEA SOUP

This soup may be served cold or hot.

SERVES 6

100 g/4 oz butter
2 onions, sliced
175 g/6 oz parsnips, peeled and cut in
  pieces
1 litre/1¾ pints strong chicken stock made
  with chicken stock cubes
225 g/8 oz frozen peas
freshly ground pepper
½ teaspoon curry powder
leaves from 1 large sprig of mint, or more
  to taste
500 ml/18 fl oz milk
120 ml/4 fl oz single cream
salt
pepper

GARNISH:
small mint sprigs

Melt the butter in a large saucepan. Add the onion and parsnip and toss around for a few minutes. The parsnip and onion must absorb the butter, but without taking colour. Pour in the stock. Cover the saucepan and simmer until the vegetables are cooked.

Add the peas and some pepper and cook for only 5 minutes more or the peas will lose colour. Let the soup cool a little then add the curry powder and mint leaves. Purée the soup in a blender or food processor and pour it into a clean saucepan. Remove from the heat, add the milk and bring the soup to a simmer. Add the cream and season to taste.
TO SERVE COLD: transfer the soup to a bowl and leave it to cool. When the soup is cold, cover the bowl and place in the refrigerator until serving time. Taste again for seasoning as the soup tends to lose flavour when it is chilled. Serve garnished with small sprigs of mint.
TO SERVE HOT: reheat the soup to boiling point and serve garnished with mint.

GREEK LEMON SOUP

This is fairly heavy soup, a quick all-in-one meal.

SERVES 4

1.5 litres/2½ pints chicken stock
350 g/12 oz short-grain white rice
juice of 1 lemon (or more to taste)
4 eggs, beaten
coarsely ground black pepper
1 teaspoon grated lemon rind

Bring the chicken stock to the boil. Add the rice and let it cook for 15 minutes. Add the lemon juice. Whisk some of the soup liquid into the beaten eggs and pour the egg mixture back into the soup. Pour the soup into a clean, cool serving bowl. Sprinkle the top with coarsely ground black pepper and the grated lemon rind.

ACCOMPANIMENTS

For a light accompaniment to soups, try bread sticks or Melba toast. Supply as well a generous bowlful of grated cheese from which guests can help themselves. Cheese will complement the flavour of any herbs in a soup.

SINIGANG NA HIPON
(SOUR PRAWN SOUP)

Sinigang broth in powdered form and nam pla are available at Asian groceries: all you need do is add water, prawns and vegetables to the sinigang broth.

SERVES 6

1.5 litres/2½ pints fish stock (see method)
  or
  sinigang broth
1 large onion, sliced
2 medium tomatoes, quartered
salt
freshly ground pepper
65 g/2½ oz white radish (mooli), cut in
  julienne
1 leek, sliced
65 g/2½ oz green beans
2 tablespoons tamarind pulp, without
  seeds
375 g/13 oz uncooked prawns, shelled
  and washed
1 tablespoon nam pla (fish sauce)
juice of ½ lemon

Make a fish stock by boiling fish heads and bones in 2 litres/3½ pints of water for about 45 minutes to 1 hour. Strain the liquid into a large saucepan and discard all the solid matter.

Bring the stock to the boil. Add the onion, tomatoes, salt, pepper, radish, leek and green beans. Boil for 5 minutes.

Soak the tamarind pulp in boiling water and strain it into the soup. Add the prawns, then the nam pla and lemon juice. The tamarind and lemon juice determine the sour flavour of the soup. Simmer for 5 minutes or until the vegetables and prawns are cooked. Serve immediately.

The contrasting flavours of Sinigang na Hipon are best when piping hot

FENNEL SOUP

SERVES 8

3 medium onions, chopped
100 g/4 oz butter
4 fennel bulbs, trimmed and sliced
2 litres/3½ pints chicken stock (chicken
  stock cubes are suitable)
2 litres/3½ pints milk
salt
freshly ground pepper
cream (optional)

GARNISH:
green fronds of fennel leaf

Using a large saucepan, sauté the onions in butter for a few minutes. Add the sliced fennel bulbs and toss them around to soften them a little. Pour in the chicken stock, cover and simmer until the vegetables are soft. Purée the soup in a blender or food processor and strain it into a clean saucepan. Add the milk, season with salt and pepper to taste and bring the soup to the boil. Taste again for salt and pepper. Add a little cream if you wish. Serve hot, garnished with fennel fronds.

STOCKS

Home-made stock is always worth the effort, and need not take hours to prepare. It can, for example, be based on a vegetable purée. In a hotly flavoured or spicy soup, Sinigang broth will provide an instant oriental flavour.

VEGETABLE STARTERS

VEGETABLE MEDLEY WITH HOLLANDAISE SAUCE

Squash, once a rarity in Britain, are now more widely available, especially from farm stalls. Use pattypan squash if baby acorn squash are unobtainable.

SERVES 4

4 baby acorn squash or sliced courgettes
100 g/4 oz mange tout
175 g/6 oz cauliflower florets
175 g/6 oz broccoli florets

HOLLANDAISE SAUCE:
2 tablespoons lemon juice
yolks of 2 eggs
100 g/4 oz unsalted butter, chilled and cut
  in pieces
salt
freshly ground white pepper

Cook the vegetables in boiling salted water. It is advisable to cook each variety separately, but using the same pan of water. Drain the vegetables well and set them aside in a warm place.

TO MAKE THE HOLLANDAISE SAUCE: beat the lemon juice and egg yolks in a small pan with a whisk and thicken them carefully, without boiling, over a low heat. Immediately beat in the butter, a small piece at a time. Season with salt and pepper to taste. Place the vegetables in a heated serving dish and spoon over some of the sauce. Serve immediately, passing the remaining sauce round separately in a small bowl.

FEUILLETÉ OF FRENCH MUSHROOMS

SERVES 4

PASTRY:
175 g/6 oz puff pastry

MUSHROOMS:
100 g/4 oz cèpes
100 g/4 oz chanterelles
50 g/2 oz morels
25 g/1 oz butter
100 ml/3½ fl oz red wine
300 ml/½ pint demi-glace sauce (see page
  75)
1 truffle, sliced thinly
a little melted butter

TO COOK THE PASTRY: roll out the pastry on a lightly floured board and cut it into four triangles. Place these on a flat biscuit tray and bake in a preheated 200°C/400°F, Gas Mark 6 oven for 18-20 minutes or until the pastry is well risen, golden and firm in the centre.

TO COOK THE MUSHROOMS: slice the mushrooms and place them in a saucepan with half the butter. Sauté until the mushrooms are soft and the liquid has evaporated. Add the wine and demi-glace sauce and cook the mushrooms.

Remove the cooked mushrooms from the sauce and keep them warm. Add the truffle and the rest of the butter to the sauce and reduce until it is rich and syrupy.

TO SERVE: reheat the pastry if necessary: cut the triangles in half and place them in a preheated 200°C/400°F, Gas Mark 6 oven for 8-10 minutes. Place the bases of the triangles on four warm plates and arrange the mushrooms on top of the pastry. Pour over the truffle sauce. Brush the pastry lids with a little melted butter, place them on top of the mushrooms and serve.

THE WHARF FOUGAFFE

MAKES 12

FOUGAFFES:
15 g/½ oz fresh yeast
4 tablespoons lukewarm water
450 g/1 lb plain flour
pinch of salt
2 tablespoons sugar
3 lightly beaten eggs
175 ml/6 fl oz lukewarm milk
100 g/4 oz lard, grated
egg wash (2 eggs beaten with 1 tablespoon
  cold water)

FILLING:
aubergine, sliced thinly and fried in olive
  oil
red and green peppers, cut into strips and
  braised in olive oil
courgettes, sliced and steamed
tomato slices
pine nuts
lettuce
salt
freshly ground pepper
250 ml/8 fl oz mayonnaise

GARNISH:
Italian parsley

The Wharf Fougaffe enfolds Mediterranean vegetables in layers of golden pastry

Dissolve the yeast in the lukewarm water and mix in 50 g/2 oz of the flour. Form the mixture into a ball, mark a cross on top and place it in a bowl of warm water. Leave it to stand until the yeast ball rises to the surface. Drain well and set aside.

Sift the remaining flour into a large bowl with a pinch of salt. Make a well in the centre. Mix the sugar, eggs, milk and yeast ball together and pour them into the well. Gradually mix in the flour and beat well. Beat in the lard.

Place the dough in a greased bowl and sprinkle the top lightly with flour. Cover it with cling film and leave it to rise overnight or for at least 6 hours in the refrigerator.

Knock the dough down and knead it lightly on a floured board. Roll out the dough to a thickness of about 2 cm/¾ inch or less. Cut out 12 squares measuring 15 cm/6 inches. Place them on a buttered baking sheet and crisscross the tops of the fougaffes with a sharp knife. Paint them with egg wash and set aside in a warm place for 15 minutes.

Bake in a preheated 230°C/450°F, Gas Mark 8 oven for about 15 minutes or until well browned.

TO ASSEMBLE: split the fougaffes in two lengthways. Mix the prepared filling ingredients with a little mayonnaise, fill the fougaffes and garnish with Italian parsley.

VEGETABLE PLATTER WITH CURRY MAYONNAISE

SERVES 6

1 × 400 g/14 oz can artichoke hearts,
   drained
3 sticks celery
100 g/4 oz green beans, trimmed
225 g/8 oz cauliflower florets
100 g/4 oz button mushrooms
2 tomatoes

CURRY MAYONNAISE:
350 ml/12 fl oz home-made mayonnaise
1 tablespoon curry powder
1 clove garlic, crushed
1 teaspoon lemon juice
1 tablespoon chopped parsley
salt
freshly ground pepper
few drops of Tabasco

ACCOMPANIMENTS:
375 g/13 oz blue cheese
375 g/13 oz ripe brie
crackers

GARNISH:
cherry tomatoes
alfalfa sprouts

TO PREPARE THE VEGETABLES: cut the artichokes in half. Cut the celery into 6 cm/2½ inch chunks. Slice lengthwise through the end of each stick a few times with a sharp knife. Place the celery in iced water for 30 minutes so that the ends will curl. Blanch the beans and cauliflower florets separately in boiling salted water for a few minutes. Drain them and refresh under cold running water. Trim the stalks of the mushrooms and wipe the caps. Cut the tomatoes in quarters. Place all the vegetables in separate, covered bowls in the refrigerator until serving time.

TO MAKE THE CURRY MAYONNAISE: whip all the ingredients together well. Pour the mixture into a bowl and place it in the refrigerator to chill before serving.
TO SERVE: place the bowl of curry mayonnaise on a large platter and arrange the vegetables around the bowl. Serve with a cheeseboard of blue cheese, brie and crackers and garnish with cherry tomatoes and alfalfa sprouts.

LEEK PAVÉ WITH GINGER VINAIGRETTE

SERVES 8

15 baby leeks, well washed to remove grit
sea salt
freshly ground black pepper

GINGER VINAIGRETTE:
2 tablespoons julienne of stem ginger
5 tablespoons peanut oil
1½ tablespoons red wine vinegar
2 tablespoons soy sauce

Line a rectangular 23 × 9 × 7 cm/9 × 3½ × 2¾ inch mould with a double layer of foil.

Trim the leeks to fit the length of the mould. Place them in a large pan of boiling water until they are only just cooked. Immediately refresh them under cold water and drain them well. (If the leeks are overcooked they will become stringy and spoil the pavé.) Arrange a layer of the leeks running one way on the bottom of the mould. Season with salt and pepper to taste and arrange a second layer on top, this time with the leeks running crossways. Add a little more seasoning. Repeat layering and seasoning in this way until the mould is full. Cover it with foil and a board that fits exactly inside the top of the mould.

With the board in place, invert the mould on a large dish and weigh it down with several heavy objects. This will eliminate the excess juices. Cover the mould with foil and refrigerate overnight.
TO MAKE THE VINAIGRETTE: whisk all the ingredients together.
TO SERVE: remove the foil covering, the weights and the board. Pour away the excess liquid. Unmould the pavé carefully on a larger board and remove the rest of the foil. Using an electric knife, trim the ends off the pavé. Cut it into 8 even slices and place them on large flat plates. Spoon a little vinaigrette over the end of each slice and serve at once.

SALAD DAYS

Increasingly, salads are served as a healthy accompaniment to a wide range of dishes or as a course in their own right. A light, appetising salad makes an excellent starter and offers plenty of scope. Freshness is the vital ingredient: all salads need to be prepared as close as possible to serving, adding dressings at the last moment. Choose crisp varieties of lettuce such as cos or iceberg, or Chinese leaves which will provide a crunchier alternative. Chicory, curly endive, lamb's lettuce or blanched dandelion leaves introduce a bitter-sweet flavour. Spinach leaves can also be blanched for a salad or, if very young, served raw. Add piquancy with freshly picked sorrel leaves or the feathery leaves of chervil and dill.

COURGETTE SOUFFLÉ

The mixture can be prepared in advance and cooked just before serving.

SERVES 6

butter for greasing moulds
2 tablespoons white breadcrumbs
350 g/12 oz courgettes, washed and
*   trimmed but left whole*
50 g/2 oz butter
1 onion, chopped finely
3 tablespoons plain flour
175 ml/6 fl oz hot milk
120 ml/4 fl oz cream
pinch of nutmeg
salt
freshly ground pepper
Tabasco
4 egg yolks
40 g/1½ oz tasty cheese, grated
2-3 tablespoons grated Parmesan cheese
6 egg whites
pinch of cream of tartar

TOPPING:
extra grated Parmesan cheese

Butter 6 × 250 ml/8 fl oz soufflé dishes or 1 x 1.5 litre/2½ pint soufflé dish and sprinkle the bottom and sides with breadcrumbs. Cook the whole courgettes for a few minutes in boiling salted water until just tender. Drain well, chop coarsely and purée in a blender or food processor.

Melt the butter in a small saucepan. Add the onion and fry gently until it is soft and translucent but not brown. Sprinkle the flour over the onion and stir it in over a low heat. Away from the heat, add the milk all at once, whisking well. Return the pan to the heat. Bring the milk to the boil, lower the heat and simmer for 2 minutes, stirring constantly. Add the cream and courgette purée. Season well with nutmeg, salt, pepper and Tabasco. Remove the pan from the heat. Beat in the egg yolks and the two cheeses.

The mixture can be prepared to this point and covered with cling film until you are ready to continue, then reheated without letting it boil.

Place a baking sheet in a preheated 230°C/450°F, Gas Mark 8 oven. Whisk the egg whites with the cream of tartar and salt until they form stiff peaks. Stir 2 tablespoons of egg white into the courgette mixture to lighten the texture. Gently fold in the remaining egg white. Pour into the prepared soufflé dishes and level the tops with a spatula. Sprinkle with the extra Parmesan cheese. Place the soufflés on the preheated baking sheet, lower the heat to 190°C/375°F, Gas Mark 5 and cook for 12-15 minutes until puffed and golden brown. Serve immediately.

STUFFED ARTICHOKES AND ANCHOVY SAUCE

SERVES 6

6 artichokes
1 tablespoon lemon juice

STUFFING:
1 tablespoon chopped parsley
1 teaspoon chopped pine nuts
1 anchovy fillet, chopped
salt
freshly ground pepper
1 tablespoon white wine

ANCHOVY SAUCE:
1 × 150 g/5 oz carton soured cream
250 ml/8 fl oz chicken stock
1 teaspoon anchovy sauce or
*   Worcestershire sauce*

GARNISH:
dried chanterelles, soaked in warm water
*   until soft*
pink peppercorns (see page 65)
saffron
red pepper, finely sliced into fan shapes

Trim the artichokes and cook them in boiling salted water until they are tender. Add the lemon juice to the water to prevent discoloration. Remove all the cooked artichokes from the water, trim off the tough outer leaves and part of the stalk. Cut them in half, paring each stalk to a tapered shape. Remove the choke if necessary.

TO MAKE THE STUFFING: combine the ingredients for the stuffing and divide it equally between the halves, spooning it into the centre of each. If you wish to eat them warm, place the artichokes in a pan in a preheated low 140°C/275°F, Gas Mark 1 oven, adding a small amount of the chicken stock for the sauce with the wine to keep the artichokes moist.

TO MAKE THE SAUCE: combine the sauce ingredients in a small saucepan and reduce until thickened. Season with salt and pepper to taste.

TO SERVE: place 2 stuffed artichoke halves on each of 6 individual plates. Spoon a small portion of sauce on one side of each plate. On to the sauce sprinkle a garnish of chanterelles, a few pink peppercorns (if using), threads of saffron and a fan of red capsicum. This dish may be served warm or cool.

In Stuffed Artichokes and Anchovy Sauce
the flavours and colours of vegetables
and herbs combine perfectly

TOMATO SOUFFLÉS

SERVES 6

6 large tomatoes
40 g/1½ oz butter
salt
freshly ground pepper
25 g/1 oz plain flour
4 egg yolks, beaten
2 tablespoons single cream
2 tablespoons grated Parmesan cheese
5 egg whites, beaten to soft peaks

GARNISH:
mint sprigs

Cut the tops off the tomatoes and scoop out the flesh. Reserve the flesh, turning the tomato shells upside down on paper towels to drain. Simmer the tomato juices and pulp with 1 tablespoon of the butter until the pulp is cooked and thickened.

Strain the pulp through a sieve to make a purée and discard the seeds. Season the purée with salt and pepper to taste.

Melt the remaining butter in a saucepan. Add the flour and cook for a few seconds. Remove the pan from the heat. Add the egg yolks, fresh tomato purée, cream and grated cheese and cook for a few more minutes, stirring constantly. Do not boil.

Incorporate 2 tablespoons of beaten egg white into the tomato mixture. Fold in the remaining egg white and fill the tomato cases with the soufflé mixture.

Place the tomatoes on a baking sheet and cook in a preheated 230°C/450°F, Gas Mark 8 oven for 5 minutes. Reduce the temperature to 200°C/400°F, Gas Mark 6 and continue to cook for 15-20 minutes altogether, until the soufflé is risen and golden.

Serve immediately, garnished with a few sprigs of mint.

TOMATO SORBET

SERVES 10

1 litre/1¾ pints fresh tomato purée
500 ml/18 fl oz sugar syrup (made with
  300 g/11 oz sugar to 300 ml/½ pint
  water)
juice of 1 or 2 lemons, according to taste
dash of Tabasco
salt

VEGETABLES:
10 firm red tomatoes, skinned
20 asparagus tips
½ small cauliflower
1 mignonette lettuce, washed
10 fresh button mushrooms
2 medium carrots, peeled and cut in fine
  julienne
2 cooked beetroot, peeled and cut in fine
  julienne
3 tablespoons mayonnaise

VINAIGRETTE:
175 ml/6 fl oz olive oil
lemon juice
salt
freshly ground pepper

GARNISH:
bunch of Italian parsley

Make the tomato purée in a blender or food processor, but do not purée the tomatoes too much or the mixture will lose colour and become milky. Press it through a sieve and discard the solids.
TO MAKE THE SYRUP: boil the water and sugar together to dissolve the sugar completely. Allow the mixture to cool.
TO MAKE THE SORBET: mix the fresh tomato purée, syrup, lemon juice and Tabasco together and season with salt to taste. Cover and place in the refrigerator to chill. Freeze in an ice-cream maker.
TO PREPARE THE VEGETABLES: cut a small slice from the top of each tomato and hollow out the centres. Turn them upside down to drain well, cover and chill in the refrigerator. Cook the asparagus tips in boiling salted water for 5 minutes. Refresh them under cold water, drain and set aside.

Break the cauliflower into tiny florets. Tear the lettuce leaves into small pieces. Remove the mushroom stems and wipe the caps with paper towels.
TO MAKE THE VINAIGRETTE: in a jar, mix together the oil and lemon juice. Season with salt and pepper to taste and shake the jar well to amalgamate the ingredients.
TO ASSEMBLE THE SALAD: place a small tomato in the centre of each individual plate. Surround each one with 2 tips of asparagus, 1 mushroom on a small piece of lettuce, a tiny pile of carrot, a tiny pile of beetroot and 2 or 3 cauliflower florets on a small piece of lettuce. Drizzle vinaigrette on to the asparagus, mushroom and carrot and spoon a little mayonnaise over the cauliflower. Fill the tomato with tomato sorbet.
TO GARNISH: strip the leaves from the parsley and arrange 1 or 2 of the leaves on the tomatoes. Serve at once.

Place an individual Tomato Sorbet in the centre of its own miniature salad, each ingredient complementing its neighbour

MIXED STARTERS

VEGETABLE AND CHICKEN TERRINE

SERVES 8

CHICKEN MOUSSELINE:
400 g/14 oz chicken breasts, chopped
2 egg whites
salt
freshly ground pepper
400 ml/14 fl oz double cream, lightly
*   whipped*

VEGETABLES:
leaves from a bunch of watercress
1 head broccoli, cut in small florets
18 French beans, topped and tailed
14 mange tout, topped and tailed
3-4 small carrots
4 small courgettes
1 × 400 g/14 oz tin artichoke hearts,
*   drained and cut in half (or 225 g/8 oz*
*   fresh artichoke hearts, cooked)*

TOMATO VINAIGRETTE:
4 tablespoons tomato purée
4 tablespoons red wine vinegar
a little sugar
salt
freshly ground pepper
120 ml/4 fl oz olive oil

TO MAKE THE MOUSSELINE: process the chicken breasts in a blender or food processor to a fine purée. Add the egg whites, salt and pepper.

Place the mixture in a cold bowl and gradually work in the cream. Refrigerate.
TO PREPARE THE VEGETABLES: purée the watercress leaves in a blender or food processor and set aside. Cook the vegetables separately in boiling salted water. Drain them

and dry. Cut the carrots and courgettes in julienne and halve the artichoke hearts.
TO ASSEMBLE AND COOK THE TERRINE: mix the watercress purée with a little mousseline and spread the mixture on the base of a well-oiled 30 × 10 cm/12 × 4 inch loaf tin. Place the carrots in the tin and cover with a layer of mousseline. Continue to layer the vegetables and mousseline until the tin is full, ending with mousseline.

Cover the tin with greased foil. Place the terrine in a baking dish and pour in boiling water to come three quarters of the way up the terrine. Bake in a preheated 140°C/275°F, Gas Mark 1 oven for 30-40 minutes. Remove the foil and, if the mousseline is not set, cover and cook a little longer. When cooked, remove the terrine from the water and allow to cool. Refrigerate for 12 hours.
TO MAKE THE VINAIGRETTE: process the tomato purée, vinegar, sugar, salt and pepper in a blender or food processor. Gradually add the oil. Taste for salt and pepper.
TO SERVE: unmould the terrine and cut into slices. Serve with tomato vinaigrette.

EAST-WEST HORS-D'OEUVRES

SERVES 8

2 or 3 lobster tails, according to size,
*   cooked and cleaned*
3 mangoes, peeled
3 avocados, peeled, stones removed

CURRY MUSTARD SAUCE:
3 teaspoons Dijon mustard
2 teaspoons Indian curry powder
2 teaspoons red wine vinegar
6 tablespoons peanut oil

GARNISH:
1 × 50 g/2 oz can truffles, drained and
*   cut in julienne*

Slice the lobster tails in medallions. You will need 2 medallions per person. Slice the mangoes and avocados thinly.
TO MAKE THE CURRY MUSTARD SAUCE: place the mustard, curry powder and vinegar in a small bowl and beat with a whisk. Gradually whisk in the oil, a few drops at a time, until the sauce is thick.
TO SERVE: use coloured plates for the hors-d'oeuvres. Place 2 medallions of lobster in the centre of each, and arrange alternate slices of mango and avocado around them as if they were flower petals. Place a spoonful of mustard sauce on the lobster.

Garnish with a few strips of truffle and serve immediately.

ASPARAGUS WITH QUAIL EGG SALAD AND CHIVE VINAIGRETTE

SERVES 8

24 quail eggs
40 stalks green asparagus, washed and
*   trimmed*

VINAIGRETTE:
1 clove garlic
250 ml/8 fl oz olive oil
250 ml/8 fl oz vinegar
salt
freshly ground black pepper
1 teaspoon English mustard
small bunch chives, chopped finely

Boil the quail eggs for 3 minutes and cool them under running cold water. Remove the shells and chill the eggs thoroughly in the refrigerator.
TO PREPARE THE ASPARAGUS: blanch the stalks in hot salted water for approximately 4-5 minutes. Refresh them under cold water and drain.
TO MAKE THE VINAIGRETTE: cut the garlic in half

and rub it around a stainless steel bowl. Add all the other ingredients and whisk for about 2 minutes until they emulsify.

TO ASSEMBLE THE SALAD: divide the asparagus stalks evenly between 8 individual serving plates in a pattern. Cut the quail eggs in half and arrange 6 halves in the centre of each salad plate. Carefully spoon over the chive vinaigrette and serve immediately.

TOMATOES VARENNE

SERVES 6

6 large ripe tomatoes, skinned and with the
    tops cut off
1 medium lobster or crab, cooked
3 cloves garlic, crushed
350 ml/12 fl oz mayonnaise
1½ tablespoons tomato purée
4 tablespoons Pernod
salt
freshly ground pepper
6 oeufs mollets (soft-cooked eggs), shelled

GARNISH:
1 tablespoon capers, chopped
1 tablespoon parsley, chopped

Scoop the seeds out of the tomatoes. Turn the tomatoes upside down on paper towels in the refrigerator to drain and chill. Slice the lobster tail and remove the meat from the claws in perfect sections. Reserve the tomalley and coral, if any. Combine the garlic, mayonnaise, tomato purée, tomalley and coral of lobster, and blend with Pernod. Season the mixture with salt and pepper to taste and set aside.

TO SERVE: place the tomatoes on individual serving plates. Put 1 oeuf mollet in each. Arrange 2 lobster pieces on either side. Dress with the mayonnaise and garnish with capers and chopped parsley.

AVOCADOS WITH PRAWN MAYONNAISE

SERVES 10

5 large avocados, peeled, halved and
    stones removed

PRAWN MAYONNAISE:
450 g/1 lb jumbo prawns, peeled and
    deveined
yolks of 4 large eggs
3 teaspoons Dijon mustard
salt
freshly ground pepper
4 tablespoons lemon juice
750 ml/1¼ pints grapeseed or peanut oil
300 g/11 oz cucumber, finely diced

TO MAKE THE PRAWN MAYONNAISE: place the prawns in a food processor with the egg yolks, mustard, salt, pepper and lemon juice. Process until the prawns are thoroughly puréed. With the motor still running, gradually add the oil until the mixture is amalgamated. Just before serving, add the diced cucumber and taste for salt, pepper and lemon juice.

TO SERVE: place half an avocado on each plate and spoon over some mayonnaise.

ROASTED GOATS' CHEESE SALAD

SERVES 8

a green salad (chicory, endive, variegated
    radicchio and so on)
2 tablespoons vinegar
salt
freshly ground pepper
6 tablespoons olive oil
50 g/2 oz butter
8 slices French bread
8 slices goats' cheese, 1 cm/½ inch thick

Heat the oven to maximum heat. Wash and prepare the salad leaves. Make a vinaigrette dressing directly in the salad bowl putting in first the vinegar, salt and pepper, and then beating in the oil. Put in the salad leaves and toss them just before serving.

Butter the bread and place a slice of cheese on each bread slice. Bake on a baking sheet on the centre shelf of the oven for 10 minutes. Serve 1 slice on each plate with a little salad.

CALAMARE IN DILL VINAIGRETTE WITH TOMATO SALAD

SERVES 2

200 g/7 oz calamare
1 tomato, sliced thinly

VINAIGRETTE:
2 tablespoons white vinegar
4 tablespoons olive oil
2 sprigs dill, chopped
salt
freshly ground white pepper

GARNISH:
sprigs of dill

TO PREPARE THE CALAMARE: remove the tentacles and outer skin and clean inside the tubes. Cut into 4 cm/1½ inch squares then, with a sharp knife, crisscross the outer skin. Blanch in boiling water for 10 seconds. Refresh them in iced water.

TO MAKE THE VINAIGRETTE: mix all the vinaigrette ingredients well in a bowl or jar.

TO SERVE: cut each slice of tomato in half. Arrange them in a circle round individual serving dishes. Place half the prepared calamare in the centre of each, season with salt and pepper to taste and dress with the vinaigrette. Garnish with sprigs of dill.

POACHED EGGS ON ARTICHOKE HEARTS WITH MOUSSELINE SAUCE

SERVES 4

4 large fresh artichoke hearts
salt
2 tablespoons white vinegar
4 fresh eggs

FILLING:
100 g/4 oz poached chicken breast
25 g/1 oz dried mushrooms, soaked for 12
   hours
2 shallots, chopped
25 g/1 oz butter
150 ml/¼ pint single cream
salt
freshly ground pepper

MOUSSELINE SAUCE:
3 egg yolks, beaten
1 tablespoon lemon juice
1 tablespoon cold water
salt
freshly ground pepper
225 g/8 oz butter, chilled and cut in pieces
100 ml/3½ fl oz whipping cream, whipped

GARNISH:
mange tout, blanched
baby carrots, blanched
chopped chives

TO COOK THE ARTICHOKE HEARTS: cook the hearts in plenty of boiling salted water with 1 tablespoon of the vinegar until they are just tender. Drain them and set aside.

TO COOK THE EGGS: carefully poach the eggs in boiling salted water with the remaining vinegar. As soon as they are ready, transfer the eggs to a shallow dish of cold water to arrest the cooking. Drain and set aside.

TO MAKE THE FILLING: dice the cooked chicken breast. Drain the mushrooms, cut them in half and wash thoroughly to remove any dirt. Sauté the shallots in the butter and add the diced chicken and mushrooms. Stir in the cream and season to taste.

TO MAKE THE SAUCE: place the egg yolks, lemon juice, water, salt and pepper in a small saucepan. Whisk them together over a low heat until the mixture thickens slightly. Beat in the butter, a small piece at a time. Stir in the whipped cream.

TO ASSEMBLE AND SERVE: gently warm through the artichoke hearts and poached eggs in a little butter in a frying pan or in a low oven. Do not let the eggs become hard. When they are warm, spoon the filling into the artichoke hearts and place a poached egg on top. Spoon over mousseline sauce and garnish with mange tout, baby carrots and chopped chives. Serve immediately.

WHELKS IN GARLIC BUTTER

SERVES 8

56 whelks or periwinkles (allow for waste)
750 g/1½ lb garlic butter made from
   crushed garlic, chopped parsley and
   butter
368 g/13 oz home-made or packet puff
   pastry, or 375 g/13 oz breadcrumbs

GLAZE:
2 eggs beaten with 4 tablespoons milk

Put the whelks in a large pan with 2 cm/¾ inch of water. Cook them for 3-5 minutes. Leave them to cool slightly. Remove the whelks from the shells with a lobster spike or crochet hook. Cut off the first part of the snail and discard it, as it is very tough.

Take 48 porcelain snail pots. Place the tail of a whelk in each one and fill the pot with garlic butter. Top each small container with a round of puff pastry cut slightly larger than the top of the pot. Glaze with egg wash. If you do not wish to use puff pastry just sprinkle the tops with breadcrumbs. Place the prepared pots on a baking sheet and cook in a preheated 230°C/450°F, Gas Mark 8 oven for 14 minutes. Serve piping hot.

TROUT AND PRAWN TIMBALES

SERVES 4

TIMBALES:
450 g/1 lb tender spinach leaves
300 g/11 oz uncooked prawns, peeled and
   cleaned
25 g/1 oz butter
salt
freshly ground pepper
2 fresh trout, skinned and filleted

SAUCE:
20 mussels
250 ml/8 fl oz white wine
1 bunch chives, chopped finely
150 g/5 oz butter
3 tablespoons crème fraîche
freshly ground pepper
lemon juice

TO MAKE THE TIMBALES: wash and blanch the spinach. Drain it well and chop finely. Cut each prawn in 4 pieces and sauté quickly with butter to seal. Season with salt and pepper to taste and combine them with the prepared spinach.

Lightly grease 4 timbale moulds and line them with the trout fillets. Fill the centres with the prawn and spinach mixture. Cover and set aside.

TO MAKE THE SAUCE: scrub the mussels and remove the beards. Steam the mussels in a large pot, with just enough white wine to cover the bottom, for about 2 minutes or until the shells open. Remove the mussels from the shells and reserve the liquor. Discard any unopened shells.

Blend the chives with the butter in a food processor or blender until the butter is a good green colour. Set aside.

Strain the mussel liquor into a saucepan. Stir in the remaining wine and crème fraîche and let the liquid reduce over a moderate heat by one third. Remove the pan from the heat and whisk in the chive butter. Season with pepper and lemon juice to taste (mussel liquor is usually quite salty). Keep the sauce warm.

TO COOK AND SERVE THE TIMBALES: steam the timbales in a covered pot over boiling water for approximately 10 minutes. Steam the mussels for 1-2 minutes to heat them through. Run a knife around the tops of the timbales and turn them out onto 4 warm plates. Scatter mussels around the timbales and pour sauce over the top of each. Serve at once.

MUSSELS WITH FRESH PEPPER

SERVES 6

2 kg/4½ lb mussels, shells scrubbed clean and beards removed
freshly ground pepper
1 teaspoon peppercorns
25 g/1 oz chopped parsley

Place the mussels in a large covered saucepan over a high heat. As soon as the mussels start to open, sprinkle them with a generous amount of freshly ground pepper plus the peppercorns, then add plenty of chopped parsley. Replace the lid and allow the mussels to cook for 3 more minutes.

Discard any that do not open. Serve them hot in their own tasty stock.

The delicate flavours of Trout and Prawn Timbales make an enticing starter

CORNET OF TROUT WITH SQUASH FLOWERS, TOMATO AND CHERVIL BEURRE BLANC

Uncooked prawns are best for cooking as the flavour is impaired if cooked twice. If baby squash are hard to come by, use courgettes.

SERVES 4

450 g/1 lb uncooked prawns, peeled and
  cleaned
2 egg whites
300 ml/½ pint double cream
salt
freshly ground pepper
2 trout, skinned and filleted
8 baby squash with flowers attached
1.5 litres/2½ pints fish stock

BEURRE BLANC:
3 tablespoons white wine vinegar
3 tablespoons water
25 g/1 oz shallots, chopped finely
salt
freshly ground white pepper
2 tablespoons crème fraîche or double
  cream
100 g/4 oz soft unsalted butter, chilled and
  cut into pieces
1 large ripe tomato, skinned, seeded and
  cut in small dice
small bunch of chervil, leaves chopped
  roughly

TO MAKE THE FILLING: place the prawns in a blender or food processor with the egg whites and cream and process until they are thick and creamy. Be careful not to over-blend or the cream will separate. Season with salt and pepper to taste. Pass the mixture through a fine sieve or mouli and place it in a piping bag fitted with a large, star-shaped tube.

TO FILL THE TROUT AND SQUASH FLOWERS: roll the trout fillets into cone shapes and pipe in some of the prawn mousse. Fill the squash flowers carefully with the remaining mousse. Place the squash and cornets of trout in a steamer and set aside while you make the beurre blanc.

TO MAKE THE BEURRE BLANC: place the vinegar, water, shallots, salt and pepper in a small stainless steel saucepan and reduce over a low heat to 1 tablespoon. Add the crème fraîche and beat in the butter, a small piece at a time. Strain the mixture and keep it warm.

TO COOK THE TROUT AND SQUASH: place the steamer over a large saucepan containing the hot stock and steam for about 10 minutes, depending on size.

TO SERVE: stir the tomato and chervil into the beurre blanc. Place 1 cornet of trout on each of 4 warm serving plates and spoon beurre blanc over the base of the cornet. Arrange 2 squash on each plate and serve immediately.

MUSSEL AND LEEK TARTS WITH SAFFRON CHAMPAGNE SAUCE

SERVES 8

PASTRY:
225 g/8 oz classic puff pastry (trimmings
  are suitable)

MUSSELS:
1.5 kg/3¼ lb mussels

SAUCE:
pinch of saffron threads
250 ml/8 fl oz mussel liquor
375 ml/13 fl oz (half a bottle) good quality
  brut champagne
600 ml/1 pint single cream

LEEKS:
3 leeks, white part only, sliced finely
100 g/4 oz butter
250 ml/8 fl oz mussel liquor

TO MAKE THE TART CASES: divide the pastry into eight 25 g/1 oz balls and roll them into thick circles. Line 8 lightly oiled 8 cm/3¼ inch tart tins with the pastry, making sure it is extended over the tops to allow for shrink-age. Cover the tart cases with circles of greaseproof paper and fill them with dried beans. Bake for 20 minutes in a preheated 230°C/450°F, Gas Mark 8 oven. Remove the beans and paper and return the cases to a turned-off or very low oven to crisp.

TO COOK THE MUSSELS: scrub and de-beard the mussels and soak them in several changes of cold water for 2 hours. Drain them and place in a large frying pan with a tight-fitting lid. Set the pan over a high heat. Give the pan a vigorous shake after 2 or 3 minutes. The mussels should have opened after 5 minutes. Discard any unopened mussels. Remove the mussels from the shells and strain the liquor through a tamis or muslin. Taste the liquor: if it is excessive-ly salty add less than the suggested 250 ml/ 8 fl oz to the sauce and to the leeks.

TO MAKE THE SAUCE: start making the sauce about 30 minutes before serving. Combine the saffron, up to 250 ml/8 fl oz mussel liquor, the champagne and cream and boil gently until reduced by half.

TO COOK THE LEEKS: sauté the leeks in melted butter. Add up to 250 ml/8 fl oz mussel liquor and boil rapidly for 5 minutes.

TO ASSEMBLE THE TARTS: fill the tarts with mussels and reheat for 5 minutes in a pre-heated 180°C/350°F, Gas Mark 4 oven. Remove them from the oven and spoon in 1 heaped tablespoon of leeks. Place the tarts on individual plates. Warm the sauce through and pour it around the mussel and leek tarts. Serve immediately.

CRAB SALAD WITH TRUFFLE MAYONNAISE

SERVES 8

MAYONNAISE:
4 egg yolks
liquid from 1 × 50 g/2 oz tin of truffles
  (reserve truffles for garnish)
salt
freshly ground pepper
400 ml/14 fl oz peanut oil
lemon juice

SALAD:
1 curly endive
4 × 1 kg/2 lb crabs, cooked
2 tablespoons dried Japanese hijiki or
  wakame seaweed, soaked in water
1 tablespoon soy sauce
4 carrots, cut in fine julienne
1 punnet salad cress
1 or 2 tablespoons Japanese rice wine
salt
freshly ground pepper
8 × size 4 eggs

GARNISH:
salad cress
chopped truffles

TO MAKE THE MAYONNAISE: place the egg yolks in a food processor. Add the truffle liquid, season with salt and pepper to taste and process together. With the motor still running, gradually pour in the oil until the mayonnaise is thick. Add lemon juice to taste.

TO MAKE THE SALAD: wash the curly endive leaves, shake off the water and put them in a plastic bag in the refrigerator.

Remove all meat from the crabs and place it in a bowl. Drain the soaked seaweed and toss it with the soy sauce over a high heat in a non-stick frying pan. Leave to cool.

Mix the crab, carrot and the leaves clipped from the mustard cress with a dash of rice wine. Season with salt and pepper and toss together.

Poach the eggs in salted water until they are set, but make sure the yolks are still runny in the centre. Drain the eggs and trim each of them to an even round shape.

TO ASSEMBLE THE SALAD: arrange the curly endive on 8 individual plates. Place the crab mixture in the centre and a poached egg on top. Spoon a little truffle mayonnaise over each salad.

TO GARNISH: sprinkle cress around the edges and garnish the salad with chopped truffles.

PRAWN CUSTARD

SERVES 6

12 medium uncooked prawns
2 shallots, chopped finely
1 teaspoon bonito flakes
2 tablespoons grated fresh ginger
6 Chinese dried mushrooms, soaked in
  water
salt
freshly ground pepper

CUSTARD:
600 ml/1 pint stock (made from prawn
  heads and shells – see method – or use
  fish stock)
3 tablespoons dry sherry
4 eggs, beaten

BEURRE BLANC:
175 ml/6 fl oz white wine
½ tablespoon finely chopped onion
1 tablespoon single cream
225 g/8 oz unsalted butter, cut into small
  pieces
salt
freshly ground pepper

GARNISH:
12 asparagus stems, steamed

Shell the prawns and boil the heads and shells with enough water to make 600 ml/1 pint stock. Remove the digestive tracts from the prawns. Wash the prawns under cold water. Cut them in half lengthways and mix with the chopped shallots, bonito flakes, grated ginger, drained Chinese mushrooms and salt and pepper. Place this mixture in the bottom of 6 × 150 ml/¼ pint moulds.

TO MAKE THE CUSTARD: beat the stock, sherry and eggs together well and pour the mixture into the moulds. Place the moulds in a roasting tin of hot water and bake in a preheated 150°C/300°F, Gas Mark 2 oven until the custard is set, approximately 45 minutes.

TO MAKE THE BEURRE BLANC: reduce the white wine with the onion until a thick, sticky syrup remains. Add the cream and bring it to the boil. Over a very low heat, beat in the butter, a piece at a time. Season to taste.

TO SERVE: unmould each custard on to a heated plate. Pour around the beurre blanc, garnish with steamed asparagus and serve.

SAVOURY TARTS

Individual puff pastry tarts (see opposite) are equally good filled with smoked haddock, poached and flaked, and generous quantities of finely chopped parsley. Make enough hollandaise sauce to coat the haddock and sprinkle with chopped parsley to serve.

SALADS

*Crisp and crunchy salads, created and dressed
with plenty of imaginative flair*

A good salad is always a success, whether as a first course, to give an appetising indication of pleasures to come, or as a refreshing side dish of mixed leaves. Main course salads are marvellous for luncheons, for informal dinners on hot summer evenings or for after-theatre suppers.

The secret of a successful salad is to prepare it as close as possible to serving time as is practical. Dressings should be added just before serving to prevent leaves going limp. However, the dressings themselves may be made in advance. Blend all the necessary ingredients in a screw-top jar and shake vigorously to amalgamate, then set aside until needed. Make sure that the lid of the jar is not metal; any vinegar in the dressing might react with this adversely, thus tainting the dressing.

Enjoy experimenting with various vinegars; balsamic vinegar, once the exclusive pride of Modena, is a must for some special dressings. Make your own herb vinegars by adding a sprig of a favourite herb – tarragon or rosemary, for instance – to a small bottle of white wine vinegar. And don't be afraid of trying different oils. It is hard to improve on the best olive oil, but take pleasure in the nuttiness of walnut and wheatgerm oils. By using your imagination and choosing from a wide range of unusual salad ingredients and garnishes – home-grown herbs, edible flowers such as borage and nasturtium – salads can be far from conventional and provide the most decorative and colourful accompaniment to your fresh and natural meals.

Imaginative salads call for a cornucopia of leaves. Salad of Mixed leaves (see page 38) incorporates lamb's lettuce and mignonette, circles of peppery nasturtium and two types of radicchio, coloured wine red or pale green flushed with pink. No meal is complete without such a centrepiece

SIDE SALADS

BREAD SALAD

This salad could also be served as a main course salad for four people.

SERVES 6

4 slices Italian bread
3 tablespoons red wine vinegar
4 cucumbers
salt
4 ripe red tomatoes
25 g/1 oz torn basil leaves
lettuce, radicchio, oak leaf or any other
*   salad leaves available*
1 red onion
120 ml/4 fl oz olive oil
3-4 drops garlic juice
freshly ground pepper
4 hard-boiled eggs, shelled and quartered

Tear the bread in pieces approximately 10 × 10 cm/4 × 4 inches, leaving the crusts on. Line the bottom of a glass bowl with the bread and sprinkle it with the red wine vinegar. Slice the cucumbers thinly, sprinkle with a little salt and leave them to stand for 20 minutes. Drain off the fluid and put the cucumbers in another bowl. Cut the tomatoes in quarters and add these to the cucumbers with the basil. Tear the salad leaves into large pieces and add them to the vegetables. Peel and slice the red onion and add it to the salad vegetables. Mix the oil and garlic juice together. Toss the salad with the oil and season to taste with salt and pepper.

Transfer the tossed salad to the bowl lined with bread. Leave it to stand for 10 minutes. To serve, toss the bread and salad and arrange the quartered eggs on top.

SPAGHETTI SQUASH SALAD

SERVES 8

1 spaghetti squash
3 avocados
juice of 1 lemon
4 tomatoes
3 tablespoons thinly sliced pomodori secchi
*   (Italian dried tomatoes in oil), drained,*
*   oil reserved*
1 cos lettuce, washed and crisped in the
*   refrigerator in a plastic container*

VINAIGRETTE:

1 clove garlic, crushed
1 teaspoon prepared English mustard
4 tablespoons white wine vinegar
good pinch of salt
freshly ground pepper
3 tablespoons oil from pomodori secchi
250 ml/8 fl oz virgin olive oil

Cook the spaghetti squash in a large covered pan of boiling salted water for 45 minutes. Drain the squash and cut it in half. Remove the seeds, and the strands of vegetable will lift out with a fork, like spaghetti. Pile them into a colander to cool.

Peel the avocados and slice each one in 8 slices lengthways. Sprinkle them with lemon juice.

Cut the tomatoes in quarters and remove the seeds. Cut the quarters in half.

TO MAKE THE VINAIGRETTE: put all the ingredients for the vinaigrette in a jar and shake it well to amalgamate.

TO ASSEMBLE THE SALAD: mix the spaghetti squash with the dried tomato and toss with a little vinaigrette. Season with salt and pepper to taste.

TO SERVE: line a round platter with cos lettuce leaves. Place the spaghetti squash salad in the centre and then arrange avocado slices and tomato wedges around the edge. Drizzle vinaigrette over the tomatoes and avocados and grind over some pepper. Serve the salad immediately.

SALAD OF TOMATOES AND BASIL

SERVES 8

1.5 kg/3¼ lb ripe, firm red tomatoes
small bunch of basil, washed
salt
freshly ground black pepper
1 clove garlic, crushed
6 tablespoons olive oil
2 tablespoons balsamic vinegar

Skin the tomatoes by dipping them in boiling water for a few seconds; the skins will come away easily. Cut the tomatoes in slices and put them in a salad bowl. Pick the basil leaves from the stems and add them to the bowl. Season well with salt and pepper and sprinkle with garlic. Pour over some oil and toss carefully. Add a little vinegar to taste and toss carefully again. Serve at once.

STUNNING SALADS

Make a *salade composée* by placing a chicory fan, a few radicchio leaves and some slices of lotus root on a plate, and call it Lotus Root, Quail Egg and Baby Corn Salad. Arrange blanched broccoli florets and mange tout, quail eggs and finely sliced red pepper in the centre and garnish with curls of spring onion.

An international variety of flavours is brought together in Lotus Root, Quail Egg and Baby Corn Salad (see page 36)

MAIN SALADS

LOBSTER AND MANGO SALAD WITH CHiLLI MINT DRESSING

Crab may be used if preferred.

SERVES 4

CHILLI MINT DRESSING:
1 litre/1¾ pints white wine
450 g/1 lb sugar
3 teaspoons lemon grass, chopped finely
½ bunch coriander, chopped roughly
a few sprigs basil
4 hot red chillies, seeded and chopped
25 g/1 oz mint, chopped finely
4 chillies, cut in julienne
175 ml/6 fl oz sesame oil

SALAD:
1 cold poached lobster
1 mango, cut in strips
4 lettuce leaves

TO MAKE THE DRESSING: place the wine, sugar, 1 teaspoon of lemon grass, coriander, basil and red chillies in a saucepan and simmer for 30 minutes. Strain and leave to cool. Pour into a screw-top jar and add the mint, chillies, remaining lemon grass and sesame oil and shake well.

TO ASSEMBLE THE SALAD: cut the lobster meat in 4 pieces. Place it on 4 individual plates with the mango strips and the lettuce leaves. Pour the dressing over and serve at once.

SCALLOP AND BEAN SALAD WITH TRUFFLE MAYONNAISE

SERVES 6

TRUFFLE MAYONNAISE:
3 egg yolks
¾ teaspoon Dijon mustard
salt
freshly ground pepper
2 tablespoons truffle juice
400 ml/14 fl oz peanut or corn oil

SALAD:
a little white wine
2 sprigs fresh dill
a few peppercorns
a little water
salt
36 fresh scallops, cleaned and trimmed
36 green beans, cut lengthways in julienne

TO MAKE THE MAYONNAISE: put the egg yolks, mustard, salt, pepper and truffle juice in a blender or food processor and process well. Pour in the oil, in a slow and steady stream, until you have a thick mayonnaise.
TO PREPARE THE SALAD: place the wine, dill, peppercorns, water and salt in a pan. Bring to the boil and simmer for a few minutes. Turn off the heat, add the scallops to the pan and let them stand for 10 minutes. Remove the scallops and drain them well (the fluid must not run into the mayonnaise when the salad is assembled).
   Cook the beans in boiling salted water for a few minutes. Drain, refresh them under cold water and drain well again.
TO ASSEMBLE THE SALAD: spoon the mayonnaise on to 6 individual plates. Arrange a portion of beans on each serving and place 6 scallops on top. Serve at once.

GADO GADO

To make coconut milk, purée 350 g/12 oz shredded coconut with 600 ml/1 pint hot water in a blender or food processor. Strain through muslin.

SERVES 6

SALAD:
2 large cucumbers, sliced
¼ cabbage, chopped roughly
275 g/10 oz beans, sliced and blanched
225 g/8 oz mung bean sprouts
1 onion, chopped in chunks
225 g/8 oz cherry tomatoes, halved

SAUCE:
1 × 50 g/2 oz jar satay sauce
500 ml/18 fl oz coconut milk

GARNISH:
3 hard-boiled eggs, shelled and quartered
100 g/4 oz peanuts
100 g/4 oz mange tout, cut in pieces

Layer the salad ingredients in a bowl. Mix the satay sauce and coconut milk together. Pour over the salad. Garnish with boiled eggs, peanuts and mange tout.

SUMMER VEGETABLES

A simple but stylish summer Salad of Mixed Leaves could include nasturtium leaves, radicchio and variegated radicchio (see page 34). Enjoy experimenting with a wide variety of vegetables.

WARM SALAD OF QUAIL WITH LARDONS AND CROÛTONS

SERVES 8

8 quail
butter for frying
salt
freshly ground pepper

SALAD GREENS:
selection of greens such as radicchio, curly
* endive, salad burnet, mignonette*

QUAIL STOCK:
quail bones
1 carrot, chopped
1 onion, chopped
1 stick celery, chopped
1 bouquet garni
500 ml/18 fl oz good quality chicken stock

CROÛTONS AND LARDONS:
8 slices bread
peanut oil
400 g/14 oz pork back fat, cut in 1 cm/½
* inch cubes*

DRESSING:
2 tablespoons sherry or red wine vinegar
2 tablespoons cold butter, cut in small
* pieces*

GARNISH:
2 tablespoons fresh herbs, chopped

Warm salad of Quail with Lardons and Croûtons includes a range of textures

Wash and dry the quail. Cut them in half with poultry shears, removing the back bones and rib bones. Set the bones aside for stock. Wash and dry the salad greens and put them in a plastic bag in the refrigerator to crisp.

TO MAKE THE QUAIL STOCK: put the bones and all the other ingredients in a saucepan. Bring to the boil, reduce the heat and simmer until about 250 ml/8 fl oz of strong, reduced stock remains. Strain the liquid into a bowl and discard the solids. Skim any fat off the top of the stock and set aside.

TO PREPARE THE CROÛTONS AND LARDONS: cut the slices of bread into small cubes and fry them in oil until they are crisp and golden. Drain them well and set aside in a warm place. Fry the cubes of pork fat in a dry pan until they are crisp. Drain them and keep them warm.

TO COOK THE QUAIL: melt the butter in a large frying pan and cook the quail pieces a few at a time. Season with salt and pepper to taste and toss them frequently so that they brown evenly. Move them around for about 6 minutes until they are quite cooked.

TO MAKE THE DRESSING: remove the quail from the pan. Pour off any fat and deglaze the pan with sherry vinegar. Add the quail stock and let it reduce until it is the consistency of syrup. Remove the pan from the heat and beat in the butter, a small piece at a time.

TO ASSEMBLE THE SALAD: cut each quail half into wing, breast and leg sections. Arrange the salad greens on a large platter. Place the pieces of quail on top and scatter over the croûtons and lardons. Spoon over some warm dressing from the pan, garnish with chopped fresh herbs and serve the salad immediately while still hot.

SALAD OF SEAFOOD 'CORDON RUBIS'

SERVES 2

SAUCE:
500 ml/18 fl oz basic lime mayonnaise (recipe follows)
1 tablespoon Worcestershire sauce
1-2 tablespoons tomato purée
Tabasco sauce to taste
1 tablespoon brandy

SEAFOOD:
fish stock or court bouillon
1 × 225 g/8 oz cutlet salmon or sea trout
1 small cooked lobster tail
10 cooked prawns
2 large freshly opened oysters

SALAD:
a few centre leaves of cos lettuce and radicchio
10 asparagus spears (optional)
a few cherry tomatoes
strips of yellow pepper or a few yellow tear-drop tomatoes

GARNISH:
freshly ground pepper
sprigs of watercress

TO MAKE THE SAUCE: whisk all the ingredients together until smooth.

TO PREPARE THE SEAFOOD: bring enough fish stock or court bouillon to cover the salmon to the boil. Place the salmon cutlet in the pan and cook for 1 minute. Remove from the heat. Let the salmon cool in the liquid. When cold, chill for 1 hour, still in the liquid. Strain, remove the skin and bones and divide the cutlet into 2 pieces. Remove the flesh from the lobster tail and slice it into 8 lengthways. Peel the prawns and remove the digestive tract from each.

TO PREPARE THE SALAD: wash and dry the lettuce leaves. Trim the asparagus spears and blanch them in boiling salted water. Drain and leave to cool. Halve the tomatoes.

TO ASSEMBLE THE SALAD: make a bed of lettuce leaves on 2 individual plates. Divide the salmon, lobster and prawns between the plates with the asparagus, pepper strips and tomatoes. Place 1 oyster beside each salad. Spoon a little sauce over each salad.

TO GARNISH: give the salads a few turns of the pepper grinder, and top with sprigs of watercress. Serve immediately, passing the remaining sauce round separately.

LIME MAYONNAISE

MAKES 600 ML/1 PINT

6 egg yolks
1 teaspoon Dijon mustard
salt
freshly ground pepper
2 tablespoons lime juice
a few drops garlic juice
250 ml/8 fl oz olive oil
250 ml/8 fl oz peanut oil
1 tablespoon boiling water

TO MAKE THE MAYONNAISE: place the egg yolks, mustard, salt, pepper, lime and garlic juice in a food processor and process until well mixed. Mix the two oils together and, with the motor still running, gradually add the oil and process until the mayonnaise is thick. Add the tablespoon of boiling water and transfer the mayonnaise to a jar. Cover and refrigerate.

VARIATION: substitute paprika for Dijon mustard, which will colour the mayonnaise soft pink, or add spice with a little mild curry powder.

Alternatively, try using half lemon and half orange juice instead of lime juice.

SALAD OF SQUID, PRAWNS AND AVOCADO

SERVES 4

40 g/1½ oz butter
1 tablespoon vegetable oil
450 g/1 lb fresh squid, cleaned and cut in thin strips
4 tablespoons chive vinaigrette (see page 28)
225 g/8 oz cooked prawns
12 asparagus spears (optional)

SALAD:
1 mignonette lettuce
1 avocado, peeled and sliced
4 carrots, peeled, cooked and cooled
4 tablespoons vinaigrette (see page 28)

GARNISH:
sprigs of watercress
chopped chives

Melt the butter and oil in a large pan. When hot, add the squid and cook it briskly, stirring all the time (squid cooks very quickly). Transfer the cooked squid from the pan to a colander and cool it under running water. Place it in a bowl, pour over 2 tablespoons of the vinaigrette and set it aside. Peel the prawns and dress with 1 tablespoon of vinaigrette. Trim the asparagus spears and blanch them in boiling salted water. Drain and leave to cool.

TO ASSEMBLE THE SALAD: wash the lettuce, dry it well and place some leaves in the centre of 4 serving plates. Top with thin strips of squid in the centre and place a few prawns around the outside. Divide the asparagus between the plates. Arrange a few slices of avocado fanning out around the squid. Make small balls of carrot with a melon scoop, toss them in the remaining vinaigrette and scatter them over the salad. Garnish with watercress and chives.

Salad of Squid, Prawns and Avocado is an ideal main course for a summer lunch

42

FISH & SHELLFISH

The catch of the season: fresh fish
that is a nutritious delight, a natural choice

Fish is a food which gives an immense amount of pleasure, not just for its flavour and texture when it is served, but also for its beautiful shape and shimmering colours before it is cooked. With so many varieties to choose from it is a worthwhile exercise to get to know a reputable fish supplier. Ask for his advice and watch him prepare seafood. There is no better way to learn how to skin and fillet than by watching an expert. Listen for recommendations on what to buy and, once in a while, experiment with an unfamiliar type of fish.

Always prepare fish when it is fresh. This is never more important than when serving shellfish. If you are buying shellfish already cooked, look for prawns with a rich colour; they tend to fade as they dry up. Look, too, for firm specimens of crab or lobster as they become limp the longer they have been on show. Never overcook shellfish as the flesh toughens very quickly.

Prepare fish simply, where possible, to make the most of its flavour; but use imaginative ways to present it, such as a plait of pollack and pink rainbow trout, with a light tomato and basil sauce, or a fan of red mullet, whiting fillets and rainbow trout, garnished with fresh asparagus and tarragon.

Keep a supply of herb butters for cooking fish: blend two tablespoons of the chopped herbs with 225 g/8 oz softened butter, add a little garlic, salt and freshly ground pepper, chicken stock and herb wine vinegar. This may be stored, wrapped in cling film, in the freezer for several months.

Of all ingredients, fish is the one whose excellence depends on freshness. Trout must be sparkling fresh; delicately coloured and flavoured, only the simplest preparations, as well as speed in cooking, are needed to make it perfect, as Truite aux Amandes (see page 52) makes plain

SHELLFISH

LOBSTER WITH VANILLA SAUCE

SERVES 4

2 × 750 g/1½ lb lobsters, freshly cooked

VANILLA SAUCE:
50 g/2 oz shallots, chopped
250 ml/8 fl oz white wine
120 ml/4 fl oz white wine vinegar
1 vanilla pod
100 g/4 oz butter, cut in small pieces

GARNISH:
2 tablespoons olive oil
10 g/⅓ oz butter
450 g/1 lb spinach, before trimming (leaves only)
2 bunches watercress (leaves only)
salt
freshly ground pepper

Remove the shells and digestive tracts from the warm lobsters and cut the flesh of each into 6 medallions. Set aside in a warm place.

TO MAKE THE SAUCE: place the shallots, wine, vinegar and vanilla pod in a stainless steel saucepan and reduce to 3 tablespoons. Strain the liquid into a clean pan and discard the solids. Beat the butter into the reduced essence, adding a little at a time.

TO PREPARE THE GARNISH: in a large saucepan, heat the oil and butter together. Add the spinach and watercress leaves and toss with salt and pepper for 3-4 minutes until they have wilted.

TO SERVE: put the cooked greens onto 4 warm serving plates and arrange 3 lobster medallions on top. Pour over the vanilla sauce and serve immediately.

SCALLOP QUENELLES WITH PRAWN SAUCE

The prawn butter used in this recipe can be made ahead and stored until you need it in the refrigerator.

SERVES 4-6

SCALLOP MOUSSELINE:
350 g/12 oz scallops
1 egg
1 egg white
¼ clove garlic, crushed
nutmeg
salt
freshly ground pepper
200 ml/⅓ pint single cream

PRAWN BUTTER:
trimmings (heads and shells) from 1 kg/ 2 lb prawns
225 g/8 oz butter, melted

SAUCE:
4 tablespoons dry vermouth
150 ml/¼ pint white wine
200 ml/⅓ pint good fish stock
300 ml/½ pint single cream
salt
freshly ground pepper
1 tablespoon prawn butter

ACCOMPANIMENT:
350 g/12 oz uncooked prawns, peeled and deveined
40 g/1½ oz butter
juice of ½ lemon
salt
freshly ground pepper

TO MAKE THE MOUSSELINE: use very cold ingredients. Blend the scallops to a very fine purée in a blender or food processor. Add the egg, then the egg white, garlic and a pinch of nutmeg. Season with salt and pepper to taste. Dribble in the cream as for a thick mayonnaise. The quantity depends on the texture of the scallops – it must hold on a spoon, so you may have to use less cream. Refrigerate for at least 1 hour. The mixture can be made several hours ahead.

TO MAKE THE PRAWN BUTTER: gently cook the prawn heads and shells in the butter for about 5 minutes. Push the mixture through a fine sieve with a pestle. Set aside to cool and leave to chill in the refrigerator. Only 1 tablespoon of prawn butter is required for the sauce. You may wish to halve the ingredients if you do not intend to store the remaining prawn butter for later use.

TO MAKE THE SAUCE: in a pan, reduce the vermouth, wine and fish stock until about 100 ml/3½ fl oz remains. Add the cream and reduce it to the consistency of a thick sauce. Season to taste with salt and pepper. Keep warm in a bain-marie.

TO MAKE THE QUENELLES: using 2 dessertspoons, take up a generous amount of the mousseline mixture in one spoon, shaping it with the other into an egg shape. Poach the quenelles gently, a few at a time, in salted water which is kept just off the boil, for 8-10 minutes. Turn them once, very carefully. Keep the remaining mixture cold. Drain the cooked quenelles well on a clean tea towel. They can be made ahead of time and gently steamed to reheat.

TO ASSEMBLE THE FINISHED DISH: cook the prawns in butter, lightly seasoned with lemon juice, salt and pepper. Arrange the quenelles carefully on heated individual serving plates with the prawns to one side. Stir 1 tablespoon of the prawn butter into the sauce and pour it around the quenelles. (Freeze any remaining prawn butter in a roll and use slices to top poached fish, if liked). Serve at once.

TAMARIND PRAWNS WRAPPED IN LEMON GRASS

SERVES 4

450 g/1 lb uncooked jumbo prawns
(available from gourmet fishmongers)
1 tablespoon instant tamarind pulp
lemon grass stalks or lemon leaves
peanut oil for frying

GARNISH:
sliced papaya
sprigs of watercress
red chillies, sliced finely

Shell the prawns, leaving the tails. Remove the digestive tracts, wash and dry the prawns. Marinate them in tamarind pulp for 5 minutes. Wrap the prawns in the lemon grass, tying it in place or skewering it with wooden toothpicks. Deep fry them in hot oil for 1 or 2 minutes.

Serve hot with slices of papaya. Garnish with watercress and sliced red chillies. Unwrap the lemon grass before eating.

OYSTERS AND CAVIAR

SERVES 2

10 large oysters
5 quail eggs
crème fraîche
sieved yolk of 4 hard-boiled eggs
2 tablespoons finely chopped chives
1 × 28 g/1 oz jar Sevruga caviar

GARNISH:
naga hijiki (Japanese seaweed)

Remove the oysters from their shells, leaving any liquid in the shell.

Boil the quail eggs for 1-2 minutes. Let

When the menu is just for two, indulge in the luxury of Oysters and Caviar

them cool, shell the eggs and cut them in half. Place half an egg in each oyster shell and cover it with crème fraîche.

Place 1 oyster in the corner of each shell. Sprinkle the quail eggs and crème fraîche with a little sieved egg yolk, chopped chives and caviar. (Lumpfish caviar can be used but sometimes it runs and this will spoil the appearance of the eggs. If you do use it, add just before serving.)

TO PREPARE THE GARNISH: toss a handful of dried seaweed into boiling water for a few minutes. Drain it and dry it on paper towels.

TO SERVE: arrange a bed of seaweed on each plate. Place 5 completed oyster shells on the seaweed and serve.

LOBSTER WITH MINT

SERVES 8

DRESSING:
juice of 3 lemons
3 tablespoons nam pla (fish sauce)
3 teaspoons sugar
2 stalks lemon grass, cut in thin slices

LOBSTER:
2 × 600 g/1¼ lb lobster tails, cooked
2 red chillies, cut in fine julienne
20 g/³⁄₄ oz very fresh mint leaves

TO MAKE THE DRESSING: mix the lemon juice, nam pla, sugar and lemon grass together.

TO COOK THE LOBSTER: remove the lobster from the shell, cut it in bite-sized pieces and place in a pot of boiling water. Stir and strain immediately. Place the lobster meat in the dressing. Toss it well and add the julienne of chillies and the mint leaves. Serve at room temperature or prepare in advance and serve cold.

HERBS FOR FISH

Freshly picked herbs are almost essential in a fish recipe. Parsley with lemon makes a near-perfect accompaniment to virtually all fish, but other herbs are rewarding too. Sorrel complements salmon and turbot, as tarragon does John Dory and plaice. Fennel enhances oily fish such as mackerel, red mullet and bass. Dill is perhaps the best accompaniment to cold shellfish.

LOBSTER WITH SAFFRON PISTILS

Dublin Bay prawns (Norway lobsters) would be delicious in this recipe. So would squat lobsters, those little-known British crustaceans, which creep into prawn creels and are sometimes available in Western Scotland and Ireland.

SERVES 2

1 lobster, weighing about 500-600 g/
1-1¼ lb, preferably alive
saffron-flavoured court bouillon

SAUCE:
15 g/½ oz shallots, chopped finely
50 ml/2 fl oz Barsac or Sauternes wine
120 ml/4 fl oz fish stock
100 ml/3½ fl oz pure cream
pinch of saffron pistils
salt
freshly ground pepper

GARNISH:
a selection of small summer vegetables,
lightly steamed

TO COOK THE LOBSTER: place the lobster in the freezer for 1 hour, then plunge it head first and with legs up into boiling saffron-flavoured court bouillon. Reduce the heat and poach the lobster for 10 minutes. Remove it from the liquid, split it in two and take out the gut and mustard. Keep warm.

TO MAKE THE SAUCE: put the shallots and wine into a small saucepan (not of aluminium) and reduce to a syrup. Reduce the fish stock and add it to the wine. Add the cream and reduce the sauce by one-third. Strain, return to the pan and bring back to the boil. Add the saffron and season to taste.

TO SERVE: place half a lobster on 2 warmed plates. Pour the sauce over the lobster and garnish with your selection of vegetables.

SPRING TOSS OF PRAWNS

These are ideal for a stylish celebration.

SERVES 20

3 kg/7 lb peeled prawns
350 g/12 oz butter
6 small chillies, cut in thin slices and seeds
removed
grated roots of 3 bunches coriander
3 tablespoons finely julienned fresh ginger
3 small cloves garlic, crushed
salt
freshly ground pepper
50 g/2 oz coriander leaves
750 ml/1¼ pints sake

SALAD GARNISH:
endive
salad cress
vinaigrette (see page 28)

Wash the prawns, drain them and remove the digestive tracts. Slice each prawn in half lengthways. Set them aside. Melt the butter in 2 large frying pans. Add half the chillies, grated coriander root, ginger and garlic to each pan and cook together for a few seconds. Throw in the prawns, season well with salt and pepper, and toss over a high heat until the prawns start to colour. Quickly add the coriander leaves and sake. Flame the sake and cook over a high heat until the prawns are just done. Spoon them on to individual serving plates and garnish with a posy of salad or a tossed green salad of your choice.

A bouquet of sharp and spicy flavours gives piquancy to Spring Toss of Prawns

LOBSTER AND PEAR SALAD

SERVES 4

1 × 1 kg/2 lb live lobster
2 small pears
50 g/2 oz sugar
1 large red tomato, skinned and seeded
1 tablespoon finely chopped chives to
*   garnish*

LOBSTER CREAM:
150 ml/¼ pint double cream
pinch of salt
freshly ground black pepper
¾ teaspoon lemon juice
4 tablespoons concentrated lobster
*   stock (see method)*

SALAD:
selected salad greens (choose 3 or 4
*   varieties of the best salad leaves, such as*
*   tender curly endive, watercress, tiny red*
*   leaves of radicchio, mâche, or lamb's*
*   lettuce, slivers of chicory or broken pieces*
*   of soft-leaved lettuce)*

DRESSING:
120 ml/4 fl oz virgin olive oil
2 tablespoons white wine vinegar
1 teaspoon Dijon mustard
¼ teaspoon freshly ground black pepper
¼ teaspoon salt

Place the lobster in the freezer for 1 hour, then plunge it head first and with legs up into boiling water. In order to make stock from the head, take the lobster from the water as soon as it has gone limp. Remove the head and place it in a pan just covered with cold water. Bring to the boil and continue to cook until 4 tablespoons of concentrated lobster stock remains. Set aside. Wrap the tail in foil and return it to boiling water for a total of 15 minutes. The meat should change from being transparent to just translucent. Cool the tail by plunging it into cold water. Remove the shell immediately. Slice the meat into neat medallions. Put them on a plate, cover with clear cling film and refrigerate.

Peel the pears and place them in a saucepan with the sugar. Add enough water to cover and boil them until they are tender. Drain the pears, cut them in half and discard the cores. Chop the flesh into dice and set it aside.

Remove the centre of the tomato. Using the outer part only, cut in to fine dice and set aside.

TO MAKE THE LOBSTER CREAM: combine the cream, salt, pepper and lemon juice in a saucepan and mix well. Whisk in the reserved concentrated lobster stock, a little at a time, then bring to boil. Cook for about 1 minute until a thickened sauce consistency is reached. Let it cool.

TO MAKE THE SALAD: wash the salad leaves and pat dry gently with a tea towel.

TO MAKE THE DRESSING: combine the ingredients in a bowl and whisk them together thoroughly.

TO SERVE: pile the dressed salad leaves at one end of the plate. At the other, place a pile of pear dice topped with lobster medallions. At each side of the plate, place a little pile of tomato dice mixed with chopped chives and a little dressing. Drizzle lobster cream over some of the medallions, salad leaves and across the plate. Finish the salad with just a scant drizzle of the seasoned cream. Serve immediately.

ZUPPA DI PESCE
(FISH SOUP)

SERVES 8

25 g/1 oz onion, chopped finely
6 tablespoons olive oil
1½ cloves garlic, crushed
3 tablespoons chopped parsley
120 ml/4 fl oz white wine
225 g/8 oz can tomatoes, chopped,
*   including juice*
500 ml/18 fl oz good fish stock
1.5-2 kg/3-4½ lb assorted firm-fleshed fish,
*   such as cod, pollack or John Dory cut in*
*   bite-sized pieces*
225 g/8 oz or more uncooked prawns,
*   peeled and deveined*
450 g/1 lb small squid, cleaned and cut in
*   rings*
8 mussels, scrubbed and beards removed
salt
freshly ground pepper

Sauté the onion in olive oil until it is translucent. Add the garlic and cook until it colours. Add the parsley and wine. Turn up the heat and when the mixture has boiled for 30 seconds, add the tomatoes. Cook for a further 30 minutes or until the oil and solids separate slightly. Add the fish stock and, when the liquid is hot, add the fish. Cook gently for 5-10 minutes, then add the prawns, squid rings and mussels. Discard any mussels that do not open during cooking. Season with salt and pepper to taste. Serve immediately with plenty of fresh bread for dipping.

The ingredients of Zuppa di Pesce may vary, depending on whatever is available fresh from the market

FISH DISHES

FISH PLAIT WITH TOMATO BASIL SAUCE

SERVES 8

TOMATO BASIL SAUCE:
5 large ripe tomatoes
1 litre/1¾ pints concentrated fish stock
350 ml/12 fl oz dry white wine
400 ml/14 fl oz double cream
3 egg yolks
40 g/1½ oz finely shredded fresh basil

FISH PLAIT:
4 fillets pollack, skinned
8 fillets pink rainbow trout, skinned
softened butter
freshly ground pepper
500 ml/18 fl oz white wine or good fish
   stock

TO MAKE THE TOMATO BASIL SAUCE: skin, seed and core the tomatoes. Cut the flesh into fine dice and set it aside. Place the skins, seeds and cores into a saucepan with the fish stock and wine and let it boil until the liquid is reduced by half. Strain it and discard the solids. Whisk the cream with the eggs. Bring the liquid back to the boil, remove the pan from the heat and whip in the cream/egg mixture. Cook over a low heat until the mixture thickens slightly. Add the diced tomatoes and basil.

TO COOK THE FISH: trim the pollack to the same length as the trout. Cut the fillets in half lengthways to make 24 strips. Cut some firm cardboard into 8 sheets of 20 × 10 cm/8 × 4 inches. Cover them with foil and butter well. Using 1 white and 2 pink strips, make plaits directly on to the foil-covered sheets.

Lay the sheets in a single layer in a roasting tin. Season them lightly with pepper and pour in white wine or fish stock. Cover the dish tightly with foil and bake in a preheated 200-230°C/400-450°F, Gas Mark 6-8 oven for 8-10 minutes, until the fish is just cooked.
TO SERVE: divide the sauce between 8 heated serving plates and slide a fish plait carefully on to the sauce. Serve immediately.

FILLETS OF WHITE FISH WITH CRAB AND LEEK SAUCE

SERVES 2

4 fillets white fish (e.g. pollack, whiting or
   John Dory), skin and bones removed
2 leeks, washed and cut in fine rings
1 tablespoon butter
salt
freshly ground pepper
120 ml/4 fl oz white wine
120 ml/4 fl oz single cream
175 g/6 oz freshly cooked crab, flaked

GARNISH:
2 crab legs

Wash and dry the fish fillets. Fold one-third of each fish back over the fillet. Soften the leeks slowly in butter for a few minutes. Place the leeks in the folded fish fillets with salt and pepper to taste. Place in a heavy frying pan with more butter if necessary, cover and cook very slowly until the fish is cooked. Remove the fish to a warm place, pour wine into the pan and reduce it to a syrup. Pour in the cream and reduce it a little again. Add the flaked crab and heat it through. Test for salt and pepper. To serve, place 2 pieces of fish on each plate and spoon over the sauce.
Garnish each portion with a crab leg.

FISH OR PRAWN BALLS WITH VEGETABLES AND BARBECUED PORK

SERVES 4

FISH OR PRAWN BALLS:
450 g/1 lb boneless fish or uncooked
   prawns, diced
100 g/4 oz pork, diced
2 egg whites
salt
freshly ground pepper
2½ teaspoons cornflour
extra cornflour for dusting
oil

VEGETABLES:
vegetable oil
runner beans cut in 5 cm/2 inch lengths
water chestnuts
small knob fresh ginger, slivered
pinch of salt
pinch of sugar
1 large clove garlic, crushed
dash of sherry
2 tablespoons oyster sauce
barbecued pork, diced

TO MAKE THE FISH OR PRAWN BALLS: place all the ingredients, except the extra cornflour and oil, in a blender or food processor and process until the mixture is smooth. Take about 1 level tablespoon of the mixture in wet hands and roll it into a ball, dusting with extra cornflour. In this way, form all the remaining mixture into balls. Allow them to set in a cool place. Fry them in hot oil.
TO COOK THE VEGETABLES: heat the oil in a wok. Toss the beans for a few moments, then add the remaining ingredients, including the cooked fish balls. Toss for a few moments. Serve when the fish balls are warmed through.

Escalopes of Salmon with Sauce Poivrade blends richness and piquancy

ESCALOPES OF SALMON WITH SAUCE POIVRADE

SERVES 6

1 large fillet of salmon, weighing about
* 1 kg/2 lb*
salt
freshly ground pepper
walnut oil

SAUCE POIVRADE (FOR 1 ESCALOPE):
a little sherry or red wine vinegar
1 teaspoon crushed black pepper
sprig of thyme
½ tablespoon veal demi-glace or very
* strong veal stock*
walnut-sized piece unsalted butter

ACCOMPANIMENT:
tender spinach leaves, steamed

Skin the salmon fillet and slice it into 6 ×
1 cm/½ inch thick escalopes. Cook only 1
escalope at a time. Have 6 heated plates
ready.

TO COOK THE SALMON: pat the escalopes with
salt and pepper. Brush a heavy frying pan
with walnut oil and put it over a high flame
until the pan is smoking. Quickly sear the
salmon on both sides. The escalopes should
be barely cooked. Put them on the warmed
plates in a preheated 110°C/225°F, Gas
Mark ¼ oven to continue cooking while
you make the sauce.

TO MAKE THE SAUCE: deglaze the pan with a
little sherry vinegar. Add the pepper, thyme
and veal demi-glace or stock. Remove the
pan from the stove and beat the butter into
the sauce. Repeat this process for each
escalope.

TO SERVE: place a few leaves of steamed
spinach on each warm plate. Arrange the
salmon on the leaves and pour the sauce
over the escalopes of salmon.

TRUITE AUX AMANDES
(ALMOND TROUT)

Truite aux Amandes is a simple, classic French dish which can be made in minutes and must be served immediately.

SERVES 4

4 × 300 g/11 oz trout, gutted and washed
salt
freshly ground pepper
plain flour
50 g/2 oz butter

ALMONDS:
25 g/1 oz butter
50 g/2 oz sliced almonds

Season the trout with salt and pepper and roll them in flour. Heat the butter in a frying pan and fry the trout gently on both sides until cooked. Remove to a heated serving platter.

TO PREPARE THE ALMONDS: melt the butter in the frying pan and fry the almonds until they are light brown. Scatter them over the trout and serve at once.

COD CARPACCIO WITH CORIANDER VINAIGRETTE, CAVIAR AND BLACK BEAN CREAM

SERVES 4

300 g/11 oz very fresh cod, sliced thinly

VINAIGRETTE:
2 tablespoons vinegar
1/2 teaspoon salt
1/2 teaspoon freshly ground pepper
120 ml/4 fl oz olive oil
2 tablespoons chopped coriander

Calamare Salad with Cucumber and Cumin is a refreshing summer dish

BLACK BEAN SAUCE:
25 g/1 oz fermented Chinese black beans
120 ml/4 fl oz fish stock
120 ml/4 fl oz double cream, whisked

GARNISH:
Sevruga or Beluga caviar

TO MAKE THE VINAIGRETTE: combine all the ingredients in a screw-top jar and shake vigorously till well mixed.

TO MAKE THE BLACK BEAN SAUCE: soak the black beans for 2-3 hours changing the water twice. Rinse the beans and purée them in a blender or food processor to a fine texture. Add the fish stock and cook very slowly for 10 minutes. Leave to cool and add the cream.

TO SERVE THE CARPACCIO: arrange the cod on cold plates. Pour some vinaigrette over each serving and drizzle some of the black bean cream sauce on top.

CALAMARE SALAD WITH CUCUMBER AND CUMIN

SERVES 20

*7 kg/16 lb uncleaned, whole small
  calamare
1.5 litres/2½ pints white wine
1 litre/1¾ pints water
2 onions, chopped coarsely
2 bay leaves*

SALAD:

*3 small cucumbers
8 spring onions*

DRESSING:

*2 tablespoons Dijon mustard
500 ml/18 fl oz crème fraîche
2 tablespoons olive oil
2 teaspoons powdered cumin
salt
freshly ground white pepper
juice of 4 limes
1 bunch mint, chopped finely
2 bunches chives, chopped finely*

GARNISH:

*4 soft-leaved lettuces
5 limes, quartered
1 bunch mint*

Clean the calamare by removing heads, tentacles, outer skin and flaps. Remove and clean the spine from each and anything else in the sac. Cut into thin rings. Bring the wine, water, onions and bay leaves to a simmer. Add half the calamare and bring to the boil. Immediately remove the pan from the heat and leave for 5 minutes. Remove the rings with a slotted spoon and set aside. Cook the remaining calamare rings as before.

TO PREPARE THE SALAD: peel the cucumbers and tunnel out the seeds. Slice across the cucumbers. The slices should be about the same size as the calamare rings. Peel and slice the spring onions into thin rings.

TO MAKE THE DRESSING: combine the mustard, crème fraîche, olive oil, cumin, salt, pepper, lime juice, mint and chives.

TO ASSEMBLE THE SALAD: carefully mix the calamare, cucumber and onion with the dressing and serve within 2 hours, at room temperature. Divide the mixture between 20 plates garnished with butter lettuce, lime quarters and a sprig of mint.

POACHED FILLETS OF DOVER SOLE ON NOODLES WITH LOBSTER MEDALLIONS AND CHIVE BUTTER

SERVES 4

*3 sole, about 500 g/1 lb each
1 cooked lobster, about 750 g/1½ lb in
  weight
a little fish stock
melted butter*

BUTTER SAUCE:

*4 tablespoons white wine vinegar
120 ml/4 fl oz white wine
2 shallots, chopped finely
1 tablespoon single cream
150 g/5 oz butter, cut in small pieces
salt
freshly ground pepper
chopped chives*

NOODLES:

*175 g/6 oz fresh noodles
50 g/2 oz (total weight) julienne of carrot,
  leek and celery
2 tomatoes, skinned and seeded
a little butter
salt
freshly ground pepper*

GARNISH:

*mange tout, cut in small triangles
tomato dice*

Fillet the sole with the skin on. Skin the fillets with a sharp knife and halve them. Remove the lobster meat from the tail and cut it in medallions. Reserve the best 4 medallions and chop the remaining lobster meat.

TO MAKE THE BUTTER SAUCE: place the vinegar, white wine and shallots in a stainless steel saucepan and simmer slowly until about 2 tablespoons of liquid remains. Strain it and return it to the pan. Add the cream and bring the liquid back to the boil. Remove the pan from the heat and, with a small wire whisk, beat in the butter, piece by piece. Add salt, pepper and the chopped chives. Set the sauce aside in a warm place.

TO COOK THE NOODLES AND GARNISH: bring a large saucepan of salted water to the boil and cook the noodles until they are al dente. Refresh them under cold water and drain. Blanch the carrot, leek and celery julienne, refresh under cold water, and drain. Cut the tomatoes in strips, reserving a little tomato for the garnish.

TO COOK THE FISH: poach the fillets of sole in a little fish stock or steam them over the stock. Place a little butter in a large frying pan and add the noodles. Toss well to warm them through. Add the carrot, leek and celery, the tomato strips and chopped lobster meat. Toss them well together and season with salt and pepper to taste.

Brush the 4 lobster medallions with a little melted butter and place them under a hot grill for a few seconds to warm through.

TO SERVE: divide the noodle mixture between 4 warmed plates, placing it in the centre. Arrange the fillets of sole on the top and place a medallion of lobster in the centre. Spoon over the butter sauce and garnish with the tomato dice and the triangles of mange tout.

GRILLED TUNA STEAKS WITH BASIL BUTTER

SERVES 4

GARNISH:
2 tablespoons olive oil
1 aubergine, sliced finely
2 red peppers baked in the oven, peeled, seeded and cut in strips
salt
freshly ground pepper

BASIL BUTTER:
100 g/4 oz butter, softened
4 tablespoons finely shredded fresh basil
salt
freshly ground pepper

TUNA:
4 fresh tuna steaks about 1.5 cm/¹/₂-³/₄ inch thick
salt
freshly ground pepper
oil for grilling

TO PREPARE THE GARNISH: heat the olive oil in a heavy frying pan and quickly fry the aubergine, a few slices at a time. Drain them on paper towels. Drizzle the pepper strips with a little olive oil and salt and pepper. Set the garnish aside to cool.

TO MAKE THE BASIL BUTTER: beat together the softened butter, basil, salt and pepper.

TO COOK THE TUNA: season the tuna steaks with salt and pepper to taste and brush them with oil. Grill them quickly under a pre-heated grill. Turn and grill the other side. The tuna should be barely cooked; too much cooking will make it dry.

TO SERVE: place a piece of tuna on each warmed serving plate. Quickly heat the basil butter and pour some over each steak. Strew with aubergine and pepper and serve at once.

JOHN DORY À LA DUGLÉRÉ

SERVES 6

1 small onion, chopped
200 g/7 oz tomatoes, chopped
6 John Dory fillets
salt
freshly ground pepper
375 ml/¹/₂ bottle dry white wine or champagne

SAUCE:
150 g/5 oz unsalted butter
75 g/3 oz plain flour
juice of 1 lemon
40 g/1¹/₂ oz parsley, chopped coarsely

Bake the onions and tomatoes in a casserole in a preheated 180°C/350°F, Gas Mark 4 oven until well cooked. Process them in a food processor and return the mixture to the casserole. Season the fish with salt and pepper to taste and place the fillets on the puréed tomato mixture in the casserole dish. Pour over the wine. Return the dish to the oven and bake until the fish is just cooked, about 8-10 minutes. Pour off any juices and reserve them for the sauce. Set the fish aside in a warm place while making the sauce.

TO MAKE THE SAUCE: melt 50 g/2 oz of the butter in a saucepan, add the flour and reserved juices, a little at a time, and cook until the sauce is smooth and has thickened. To finish the sauce, remove the saucepan from the heat. Cut the remaining butter into small pieces and beat them into the sauce one at a time. Add the lemon juice and coarsely chopped parsley. Pour the sauce over the fish and serve at once.

FRESH FISH STEAKS WITH AROMATIC VEGETABLES AND HERBS

SERVES 6

6 thick, trimmed steaks of cod or ling, each weighing about 300 g/11 oz
200 g/7 oz smoked salmon, cut in thin strips
olive oil
freshly ground pepper

GARNISH:
1 red pepper, 1 green pepper, 1 small courgette, 6 large mushrooms, all cut into fine julienne
150 g/5 oz broad beans, shelled and peeled
50 g/2 oz unsalted butter
small leaves of Italian parsley

SAUCE:
4 tablespoons jellied fish stock
2 tablespoons tomato concassé (fresh tomato sauce)
2 tablespoons soy sauce or to taste
50 g/2 oz unsalted butter

TO PREPARE THE FISH: with a sharp knife, make tiny incisions in the cod or ling steaks and fill the incisions with the strips of smoked salmon, pushing them well into the fish so the flavour penetrates during cooking.

TO PREPARE THE GARNISH: in a pot of rapidly boiling salted water, cook separately the peppers, courgette, mushrooms and broad beans for 1-2 minutes. Refresh them under cold running water to set the colour. The vegetables should remain crisp. Drain them well and set aside.

TO MAKE THE SAUCE: in a saucepan, combine the fish stock, tomato concassé and soy sauce. Bring it to the boil, cook for a few seconds and whisk in the butter, a little at a time. Remove the pan from the heat

In Pochouse, steaming the fillets helps to retain their light texture

the butter to heat through.

TO SERVE: pour a little of the sauce on each of 6 warmed plates and place the steaks in the centre. Carefully spoon some vegetable garnish on top of the fish and top with a few leaves of Italian parsley. Serve immediately.

POCHOUSE

SERVES 4

120 ml/4 fl oz white wine
1 trout, cleaned
1 large whiting, scaled and cleaned
225 g/8 oz butter, cut in small dice
1 tablespoon chopped dill
1 tablespoon salmon roe (optional)

GARNISH:
sprigs of dill

Pour the white wine into a fish kettle and steam the fish. As soon as both are ready, lift out the fillets and remove the skin. Set the fish fillets aside to keep warm. Reduce the fumet from cooking the fish until a quarter remains. Strain and discard the solids.

Beat in the butter with a whisk to make a sauce of a light, frothy consistency. Add the chopped dill or, if liked, divide the sauce into two and add chopped dill to half the sauce and salmon roe to the remainder.

TO SERVE: If using two sauces, pour dill sauce on one side of each plate and salmon roe sauce on the other. Place the whiting carefully on the dill sauce and the trout on the salmon roe sauce. If salmon roe is not added to half the sauce, cover the middle of each plate with the dill sauce. Place the trout and whiting side-by-side in the centre.

Garnish with a sprig of dill placed between the fillets and serve immediately.

and keep it warm. The sauce cannot be reheated.

TO COOK THE FISH: pour a little olive oil in a large non-stick frying pan and heat nearly to smoking point. Pepper the fish. Put in 2 or 3 fish steaks at a time and cook them quickly, for about 2-3 minutes on each side. The fish should be only just cooked and browned slightly.

While the fish is cooking, melt the 50 g/ 2 oz of butter for the garnish in a separate frying pan and toss the vegetables around in

55

SILLISALAATTI

(HERRING SALAD)

In this recipe the vegetables are peeled after they have been cooked as this helps to keep them firm, giving you more perfectly cut dice.

SERVES 4

2 beetroot, cooked and cooled
1 tablespoon vinegar
2 medium carrots, cooked and cooled
2-3 potatoes, cooked and cooled
1 apple
2 dill pickles
1 Bismarck herring fillet
2-3 spring onions

SAUCE:
250 ml/8 fl oz soured cream
pinch of sugar
salt
freshly ground pepper

TO SERVE:
lettuce leaves
1 hard-boiled egg, shelled and chopped

Peel the beetroot, cut them in 2 cm/¾ inch dice and let them stand in the vinegar for a few minutes. Peel the carrots, potatoes and apple and cut them in small cubes. Cut the pickles and herring fillet in cubes. Chop the spring onions finely.

Mix a little vinegar from the beetroot with soured cream to tint it pink. Add a pinch of sugar and season with salt and pepper to taste. Set the sauce aside.

Mix the beetroot and all the other ingredients together gently. To serve, make a lettuce cup from the leaves on each serving plate. Fill the cups with the mixture and strew chopped hard-boiled egg on top. Serve the sauce separately.

TRUITE FARCIE AU SAUMON FUMÉ

(RAINBOW TROUT FILLED WITH SMOKED SALMON MOUSSELINE AND SORREL SAUCE)

SERVES 6

6 fresh rainbow trout weighing 300 g/
* 11 oz each, cleaned and gutted with*
* head and tail intact*

MOUSSELINE:
175 g/6 oz smoked salmon, chilled
175 g/6 oz fish fillets: bass, John Dory, sea
* bream or any white fish*
1 egg
1 egg white
500 ml/18 fl oz double cream, chilled
salt
freshly ground pepper
pinch of nutmeg

SAUCE:
10-12 sorrel leaves
1 tablespoon butter
4 tablespoons dry vermouth
375 ml/13 fl oz single cream
salt
freshly ground pepper
lemon juice

TO BONE THE TROUT: slide a small, sharp, paring knife inside the trout from head to tail along each side of the collar bone. Remove the collar bones with a pair of scissors. Slide the knife between the flesh and the rib cage bones on both sides of the fish, taking care not to damage the flesh. Remove the side bones.

TO MAKE THE MOUSSELINE: place all the ingredients except the cream and seasoning in a blender or food processor one at a time, and process for 2 or 3 seconds between each addition. With the motor still running, add the cream slowly until it is well combined. Be careful not to overprocess it or the mixture will curdle. Add salt, pepper and nutmeg to taste.

TO STUFF THE FISH: fit a piping bag with a wide tube and fill it with mousseline. Lightly season the cavity of each trout with salt and pepper and pipe the mousseline into the cavity. Oil 6 sheets of greaseproof paper. Place a trout on the oiled side of each sheet and wrap the sheet around the fish forming neat parcels. Place them on a baking sheet in the refrigerator until you are ready to cook them.

TO MAKE THE SAUCE: wash the sorrel leaves and shred them. Melt the butter in a saucepan and add the sorrel, cooking it briskly to evaporate the moisture. Add the vermouth and simmer to reduce the volume by half. Pour in the cream and simmer for a few minutes more until a sauce consistency is achieved. Adjust the seasoning with salt and pepper and a few drops of lemon juice.

TO COOK AND SERVE: preheat the oven to 200°C/400°F, Gas Mark 6. Place the trout parcels in a roasting tin with hot water a quarter of the way up their sides. Place the tin in the oven and poach the fish for 10-15 minutes. While the trout are cooking, carefully reheat the sauce. When the trout are cooked, unwrap them and remove the skin, being careful not to tear the fish. Place each fish on a warmed plate and coat with sauce. Garnish with a sprig of dill and serve immediately.

The splendour of Truite Farcie au Saumon Fumé calls for simple presentation for greatest effect

GRILLED TUNA NIÇOISE

Salad dressings are usually made in the ratio of one part vinegar to two parts oil. Flavour with herbs, mustard or garlic.

SERVES 8

750 g/1¾ lb tuna fillet in one piece
450 g/1 lb of the tiniest boiling potatoes
 you can find
450 g/1 lb haricots verts or other small
 tender green beans
2 sweet red peppers roasted over an open
 flame, peeled and seeded and cut into
 5 mm/¼ inch strips
tender baby lettuces of your choice
16 olives marinated in a little sliced garlic,
 fresh thyme and olive oil

MARINADE:
2 tablespoons mild olive oil
sprigs of your favourite fresh herbs
salt
freshly ground pepper

TO ROAST POTATOES:
1 bay leaf
3 sprigs fresh thyme
3 whole garlic cloves, unpeeled
salt
freshly ground pepper
1-2 tablespoons olive oil

VINAIGRETTE FOR BEANS, POTATOES AND TUNA:

4 shallots, minced
120 ml/4 fl oz full-flavoured olive oil
1 tablespoon red wine vinegar
1 tablespoon sherry or red wine vinegar
1 tablespoon lemon juice
salt
freshly ground black pepper
4 anchovies, cleaned and chopped

VINAIGRETTE FOR PEPPERS:
fruity olive oil
a few drops of good quality balsamic
 vinegar
salt

VINAIGRETTE FOR LETTUCES:
mild olive oil
small amount of vinegar
salt

GARNISH:
edible flowers of your choice
12 croûtons of good quality crusty French
 bread, brushed with olive oil, grilled over
 an open fire and rubbed with a garlic
 clove

Trim the tuna of any dark meat near the backbone. Mix the ingredients for the marinade in a shallow dish, add the tuna, rubbing the flavoured oil into the fish, and marinate for at least 2 hours.

TO ROAST THE POTATOES: place the potatoes, herbs, garlic cloves, salt, pepper and a little olive oil in a tightly covered shallow casserole and bake in a preheated 200°C/400°F, Gas Mark 6 oven until they are tender. While the potatoes are roasting, make the vinaigrette for the beans, potatoes and tuna by combining all the ingredients except the anchovies. Prepare the vinaigrettes for the capsicums and lettuces by separately combining the ingredients for each. When the potatoes are cooked dress them with 2 tablespoons of the vinaigrette while still warm. If they are more than 2.5 cm/1 inch in diameter, cut them in halves or quarters.

TO PREPARE THE BEANS AND PEPPERS: blanch the beans in plenty of boiling salted water and refresh them in iced water. Set aside. Do not dress them until just before serving or they will lose their lovely bright green colour. Dress the strips of pepper with the olive oil and balsamic vinegar. Season.

TO COOK THE TUNA: season the tuna with salt and pepper, grill it over a medium hot flame as you would a thick beef steak until the inside of the fillet remains just rare. It will continue to cook after it is removed from the grill, so do not overcook it.

TO ASSEMBLE THE FINISHED DISH: dress the beans with half the vinaigrette. Add chopped anchovies to the remainder and set it aside to spoon over the tuna. Dress the lettuces with their vinaigrette. Slice the tuna on the diagonal as you would a thick beef steak, into 8 equal slices. Arrange the slices of tuna, olives, bean, potato and pepper salads on a serving platter or on individual plates. Spoon anchovy vinaigrette over each portion of tuna.

Garnish the plates with edible flowers such as nasturtium petals, borage flowers or mustard blossoms. Serve immediately with garlic croûtons.

ESCALOPES OF SEA TROUT WITH LIME SABAYON SAUCE ON A BED OF LEEK AND CARROT JULIENNE

SERVES 6

6 leeks (white and pale green part only)
butter

LIME SABAYON:
4 egg yolks
juice of 2 limes
salt
freshly ground pepper

TROUT:
6 escalopes of sea trout (cut from the fillets)
salt
freshly ground pepper
butter/oil

GARNISH:
2 carrots, cut in julienne
30 mange tout, cut in diamonds

Cut the leeks in fine rings. Place them in a little melted butter and sauté gently until they are cooked. Set aside in a warm place.
TO MAKE THE SABAYON SAUCE: beat the egg yolks in a stainless steel bowl and add the lime juice. Season to taste with salt and pepper. Whisk the mixture over a saucepan of warm water until it is light and fluffy and has thickened a little. Set aside in a warm place.
TO COOK THE TROUT: season the escalopes with salt and pepper and cook them in a little butter and oil in a non-stick pan.
TO COOK THE GARNISH: blanch the julienne of carrot and mange tout separately in boiling water for 3-4 minutes.
TO SERVE: place a bed of leeks on each warm dinner plate and place the escalopes of sea trout on top. Spoon over some lime sabayon. Garnish with carrot strips and mange tout diamonds.

FISH STOCK

There is no substitute for inexpensive home-made fish stock in fish soups and sauces. Almost any variety of fish can be used to make a stock. The trimmings of white fish are particularly suitable, and turbot or sole fumets are rich in gelatine for a thicker stock. Fish stock does not keep well, and is best used the day you make it, but freshwater fish stock can be frozen for later use.

FISH FANS

SERVES 8

FISH STOCK:
1 large red snapper head
2 tablespoons peanut oil
1 tablespoon butter
1 small onion, sliced finely
100 g/4 oz button mushrooms, sliced finely
2 spring onions, chopped
250 ml/8 fl oz dry white wine
1.5 litres/2½ pints cold water
6 whole black peppercorns
fresh bouquet garni (piece celery, parsley, bay leaf, thyme, tied together with cotton)

FISH:
4 whole red mullet
8 rainbow trout fillets
8 whiting fillets
butter
freshly ground pepper
1 large carrot, cut in julienne
4 asparagus spears, cut in julienne
salt

SAUCE:
1 litre/1¾ pints fish stock
500 ml/18 fl oz single cream

GARNISH:
1 bunch fresh tarragon

TO MAKE THE STOCK: sauté the fish head in the oil and butter and add the vegetables. Cook gently for 5 minutes. Add the wine and boil until it is almost evaporated. Add the cold water, peppercorns and bouquet garni. Simmer, uncovered, for 20 minutes. Skim the liquid from time to time. Strain, cover and leave to cool.
TO PREPARE THE FISH: fillet the mullet, retaining the skin for colour. Halve the trout fillets

Fish Fans present a trio of flavours

lengthways and skin them. Skin the whiting fillets. Remove the fish bones with tweezers.
Butter a baking sheet and sprinkle it with ground black pepper. Arrange the fillets in 8 fan shapes. Blanch the julienne of vegetables in separate saucepans. Refresh them by plunging them into iced water. Drain, toss the vegetables together and arrange them over the prepared fish fans. Season with salt and pepper.
TO MAKE THE SAUCE: measure 1 litre/1¾ pints of the fish stock and reduce in a pan to a brown and syrupy consistency. Add the cream, simmer gently and let the sauce reduce again until it coats the back of a wooden spoon. Set aside in a warm place.
TO COOK THE FISH: bake the fish fans in a preheated 200°C/400°F, Gas Mark 6 oven for 8 minutes. Carefully place a fish fan on each plate. Serve with the hot sauce and garnish with sprigs of fresh tarragon.

MEAT & POULTRY

*A **fresh** approach to quality meat and poultry:*
lean, simple and naturally delicious

Meat is traditionally the basis for a main course. Whatever its detractors may say, it is a prime source of nutrition, providing much of our daily vitamin and mineral requirements. It makes sense, as with all foodstuffs, to obtain the best quality available and, because of the high cost of meat, it is even more essential to find a first class butcher to advise you on the many choices of cut and to prepare and trim cuts as required. Some of the cuts in these recipes, such as rib-eyes, may be unfamiliar. A good butcher should be able to supply them.

The full flavour of meat is preserved best in cooking if it is grilled or roasted. Both methods need a minimal amount of additional fat. White meat, such as chicken, has less fat than red meat as a rule, but any surplus fat should be trimmed away.

Many cuts of meat lend themselves to rich sauces. To lighten a sauce without losing flavour, wherever possible use the meat juices as the main ingredient for the sauce with little or no thickening. Unless a sauce is a feature of presentation, serve it separately and allow guests to help themselves.

Sauces and garnishes should make full use of seasonal ingredients, as do those used in Feuilleté of Rabbit, served with a fresh green pea purée and a sorrel sauce, or Lamb Rib-eye Fleur-de-Lis garnished with fresh rosemary and apple or clusters of blackcurrants. Don't overcook meat and try a variety of vegetable or fruity stuffings. In the following recipes courgettes and fresh dates have both been used. Delicious, naturally.

Contemporary tastes call for a new attitude to the presentation of meat. Perfect individual cuts must not be overwhelmed by fuss and ostentation; accompany them with light sauces and crisp vegetables. Côte de Boeuf with Aïoli and Individual Rosti (see pages 69-70) epitomises this style

POULTRY AND GAME

KOTOPOULO AVGOLEMONO
(CHICKEN WITH LEMON SAUCE)

SERVES 2

1 × 1.25 kg/2½ lb chicken
1 onion, chopped
1 teaspoon ground cumin
salt
freshly ground pepper
100 g/4 oz butter, melted

FRIED AUBERGINE:
1 aubergine, sliced thinly lengthways
olive oil
1 clove garlic, crushed
salt
freshly ground pepper

SAUCE:
25 g/1 oz butter
2 tablespoons plain flour
500 ml/18 fl oz chicken stock
1 teaspoon paprika
1 large clove garlic, crushed in a little oil
2 tablespoons dry Vermouth
salt
freshly ground pepper
2 thin slices lemon
2 slices green pepper, chopped
120 ml/4 fl oz double cream
1 egg yolk, beaten

COUSCOUS:
100 g/4 oz couscous
salt
175 ml/6 fl oz boiling chicken stock
50 g/2 oz butter

ACCOMPANIMENTS:
couscous, boiled rice or pasta, aubergine

TO ROAST THE CHICKEN: place the chicken on the chopped onion in a baking dish. Sprinkle it with cumin and season with salt and pepper to taste. Pour over the melted butter. Roast the chicken in a preheated 190°C/375°F, Gas Mark 5 oven for 1 hour, basting frequently with the juices from the baking dish. While the chicken is cooking, cook the aubergine and make the sauce.

TO FRY THE AUBERGINE: fry the slices of aubergine in olive oil and garlic until pale brown. Season to taste with salt and pepper.

TO MAKE THE SAUCE: melt the butter in a heavy-bottomed saucepan. Add the flour, mix well and cook for 2 or 3 seconds. Pour in the chicken stock and stir until the sauce thickens. Add the paprika, garlic and Vermouth and season with salt and pepper to taste. Cut the rind off the lemon slices and discard the rind from 1 slice. Finely chop the lemon pulp and remaining rind and add to the sauce with the chopped pepper. Return the sauce to the heat and bring it to the boil. Add the cream. Pour a little sauce on to the egg yolk, mix it well and return it to the sauce in the pan. Do not cook after adding the egg or the sauce will curdle.

COUSCOUS: place 100 g/4 oz of couscous in a bowl with a pinch of salt and pour in 175 ml/6 fl oz of boiling chicken stock. Allow to stand until all the water is absorbed (1-3 minutes). Melt some butter in a large frying pan and cook the couscous over a moderate heat for 4-5 minutes, stirring constantly.

TO SERVE THE CHICKEN: halve the chicken and remove the ribs and backbone. Place a small serving of couscous and rice or pasta on each plate and place the chicken on top, skin side up. Pour over the sauce. Serve with slices of fried aubergine.

POACHED CHICKEN ON LEEKS WITH A PEAR AND GINGER CONFIT

SERVES 4

PEARS AND LEEKS:
2 small pears
2 medium leeks
50 g/2 oz butter
250 ml/8 fl oz single cream
salt
freshly ground pepper

GINGER GLAZE:
2 teaspoons sugar
2 tablespoons water
1 cm/½ inch piece fresh ginger

SAUCE:
500 ml/18 fl oz beef stock
250 ml/8 fl oz port
25 g/1 oz European dried mushrooms, soaked in beef stock for 2 hours and drained
100 g/4 oz butter, cut in small pieces

CHICKEN:
4 large chicken breasts
250 ml/8 fl oz chicken stock

ACCOMPANIMENT:
creamed potato

TO PREPARE THE PEARS AND LEEKS: peel, halve and core the pears and poach them gently in water until just tender. Refresh them in iced water and put aside.

Wash the leeks under cold running water. Cut them into 1 cm/½ inch dice. Cook them in butter for 10 minutes until soft but not coloured. Stir in the cream. Continue to cook until the mixture has thickened. Season with salt and pepper to taste. Keep the mixture warm over hot water until ready to serve.

TO MAKE THE GINGER GLAZE: caramelise the sugar and water. Peel and purée the ginger. Add it to the caramel and reduce the mixture to a glazing consistency.

TO MAKE THE SAUCE: in a pan, combine the beef stock, port and the drained, presoaked mushrooms. Reduce the sauce to 120ml/ 4 fl oz and whisk in the butter, a little at a time, over a very low heat.

TO COOK AND SERVE THE CHICKEN: poach the chicken breasts gently in chicken stock until just cooked and still tender. Place the pear halves in a baking tray and spoon over the ginger glaze. Bake in a preheated 190°C/ 375°F, Gas Mark 5 oven for 5 minutes.

Reheat the leeks and spoon on to 4 serving plates. Place a chicken breast on the leeks and spoon over the sauce. Arrange the pear and ginger confit alongside. Serve with puréed potatoes placed under a grill to brown.

Poached Chicken on Leeks with Pear and Ginger Confit and puréed potatoes

CHICKEN SATAYS WITH PEANUT SAUCE

SERVES 6

6 boneless half chicken breasts

MARINADE:
225 ml/8 fl oz coconut milk (see page 38)
1 teaspoon turmeric powder
¾ teaspoon curry powder
1 teaspoon salt

DIPPING SAUCE:
½ × 200 g/7 oz packet creamed coconut cream
120 ml/4 fl oz single cream
2 tablespoons panaeng paste (recipe follows)
3 tablespoons crunchy peanut butter
salt
sugar

Slice each chicken breast, across the grain, into 15 strips. Mix all the ingredients for the marinade together and marinate the chicken for 1-2 hours.

TO MAKE THE DIPPING SAUCE: heat the creamed coconut cream in a frying pan until the oil runs. Stir in the cream. Add the panaeng paste and cook for a few minutes. Add the peanut butter and salt and sugar to taste.

TO COOK THE SATAYS: thread 3 strips of chicken breast on each of 30 bamboo satay skewers and grill them for a few minutes.

Do not overcook them or the chicken will be dry and tough. Serve immediately with the dipping sauce.

PANAENG PASTE

10 dried chillies, cut in pieces and soaked in water until soft
1 stalk lemon grass, sliced finely
1 teaspoon chopped lime rind
10 roots coriander, chopped
7 cloves garlic, chopped
1 shallot, chopped
10 peppercorns
1 teaspoon shrimp paste

Place all the ingredients in a blender and purée until the mixture is a fine paste. If not to be served immediately, place the paste in a covered container and store it in the refrigerator.

DUCK BREASTS WITH GINGER

Dinner for twenty can be just as easy to make as dinner for ten if you choose a recipe that is simple to prepare.

SERVES 20

STOCK:
10 duck carcasses
a little oil
1.25 kg/2½ lb carrots, chopped
2 litres/3½ pints brown veal stock
1.25 litres/2¼ pints red wine
fresh bouquet garni
10 peppercorns

SAUCE:
300 g/11 oz sugar
250 ml/8 fl oz water
*250 ml/8 fl oz ginger syrup from a jar of
   stem ginger*
stock
salt
freshly ground pepper
10 knobs stem ginger, cut in fine slivers
100 g/4 oz butter, cut in small pieces

DUCK BREASTS:
20 × 150 g/5 oz duck breasts
salt
freshly ground pepper

Duck Breasts with Ginger make an impressive dish for a large number of guests

TO MAKE THE STOCK: crush the duck carcasses with a meat mallet or cleaver and brown them well in a shallow pan with a little oil. Transfer them to a stock pot with a slotted spoon. Brown the carrots well in the same shallow pan and transfer them to the stock pot in the same way. Pour the veal stock on to the duck carcasses and vegetables and deglaze the frying pan with the wine. Pour the wine into the stock pot. Add the bouquet garni and peppercorns. Bring to the boil, uncovered, reduce the heat and simmer for 45 minutes, skimming off the scum as it rises. Strain the stock and, discarding the solids in the strainer, strain the stock again, this time through 2 thicknesses of damp muslin.

TO MAKE THE SAUCE: make a caramel from the sugar and water and cook it until it is dark brown. Quickly add the ginger syrup and stock, being careful not to burn your hands in the process. Reduce the sauce to a syrup; season with salt and pepper to taste, add the slivers of ginger, and beat in the butter, a piece at a time.

TO COOK THE DUCK BREASTS: lightly score the skin of the duck breasts to allow the fat underneath to escape. Season well. Place a heavy roasting tin in the oven and preheat it to 230°C/450°F, Gas Mark 8. Place the breasts in the heated tin, skin side down, and cook in the oven for approximately 4 minutes. Turn them over and cook for a further 4 minutes. Remove the breasts from the tin and leave to rest in a warm place on a plate inverted over a larger plate to drain the juices.

TO SERVE: place the breasts on individual heated plates. Serve with the heated sauce and a selection of vegetables of your choice.

CHICKEN FILLETS IN PINK PEPPERCORN AND BRANDY SAUCE

SERVES 6

plain flour
salt
freshly ground pepper
6 boneless chicken breasts
2 tablespoons butter
2-3 tablespoons concentrated chicken stock or 2 chicken stock cubes
1½ tablespoons pickled pink peppercorns (see right), drained
120 ml/4 fl oz brandy
350 ml/12 fl oz single cream

Season the flour with salt and freshly ground pepper. Toss the chicken breasts in the flour and shake off the excess. Heat a frying pan, add the butter and fry the chicken breasts quickly, slightly browning each side. Reduce the heat, and stir in the chicken stock or crumbled cubes and the pink peppercorns. Pour in the brandy. Ignite the brandy, and, when the flames have subsided, stir in the cream. Simmer on a very low heat for 5 minutes. Serve with Swedish Potatoes, Honeyed Buttered Carrots and Broccoli with Lemon Butter (recipes follow).

SWEDISH POTATOES

SERVES 6

3 large potatoes
paprika
salt
melted butter

Peel the potatoes. Wash and dry them well with paper towels. Cut each potato in half lengthways. Slice through the rounded side of the potato halves crossways at approximately 1 cm/½ inch intervals, making sure not to cut right through. Place the potatoes on a greased baking dish and sprinkle with paprika and salt. Bake in a preheated 190°C/375°F, Gas Mark 5 oven for 1-1¼ hours until the potatoes are brown and tender, frequently brushing them with melted butter as they cook.

HONEYED BUTTERED CARROTS

SERVES 6

4 medium carrots
salt
1½ tablespoons honey
25 g/1 oz butter
freshly ground pepper

Peel the carrots and slice them thinly on the diagonal. Place them in a saucepan of boiling water with ¼ teaspoon salt. Cook them for a few minutes until they are tender but still crisp. Drain the carrots. Toss them immediately, while they are still hot, with honey and butter. Season to taste with salt and pepper.

BROCCOLI WITH LEMON BUTTER

SERVES 6

1 kg/2 lb broccoli florets
50 g/2 oz butter
2 tablespoons lemon juice

Trim the tough ends of the broccoli and make crossways slits in the bases of the stems. Stand the broccoli upright in a saucepan containing a little lightly salted water. Cover the pan and cook until the stalks are just tender (about 12-15 minutes). Drain and keep warm. Melt the butter in a small saucepan, add the lemon juice and bring to the boil. Pour over the broccoli and serve at once.

PEPPERCORNS

Pepper is probably the most widely used spice. It is best if freshly ground, as the flavour deteriorates after grinding. White peppercorns are fully ripe berries from which the outer hull has been removed, and they are quite hot. Black peppercorns are milder, picked while still green and dried out till they become dark brown or black. Green peppercorns are also picked before ripening and are preserved in brine; they are soft enough to grind into a paste, and are the mildest of all. Pink or red peppercorns come from a different plant and can cause an allergic reaction. If you can eat them, enjoy them for their colour and piquancy; if you can't, use white or black ones instead.

POUSSINS FILLED WITH SPICED BLACK RICE

SERVES 6

6 × 350 g/12 oz poussins
salt
freshly ground pepper
50 g/2 oz melted butter

FILLING:
150 ml/¼ pint vegetable oil
200 g/7 oz shallots
450 g/1 lb black glutinous rice
2 cinnamon sticks
1 tablespoon cumin seeds
1 teaspoon fenugreek
4 bay leaves
2 litres/3½ pints water
4 sticks celery, chopped
1 bunch chives, chopped
grated rind of 1 orange
salt
freshly ground pepper

SAUCE:
½ teaspoon crushed garlic
½ teaspoon chopped fresh chilli
2 teaspoons tamari (Japanese soy sauce)
150 g/5 oz butter, cut in small pieces

Bone the poussins through the back, leaving the wings and legs intact. Season.

TO MAKE THE FILLING: heat the oil in a frying pan. Add the shallots and sauté them until soft. Add the black rice and stir until it is well coated with oil. Add all the spices and cover with water. Bring to the boil, reduce the heat and simmer for about 40 minutes, stirring occasionally and adding more water if necessary. The rice is cooked when it is no longer firm and the mixture is sticky. Leave it to cool. Add the celery, chives and orange rind and season with salt and pepper to taste.

TO STUFF THE POUSSINS: lay each poussin skin side down on a board and fill the open cavity with spiced black rice. Sew or skewer the back edges together. Brush the skin of each poussin with butter. Place them in a roasting tin and bake in a preheated 230°C/450°F, Gas Mark 8 oven for approximately 20-25 minutes. Set them aside in a warm place to rest for 20 minutes.

TO MAKE THE SAUCE: over a high heat reduce the pan juices with the garlic, fresh chilli and soy sauce. Beat in the butter, a piece at a time. Serve the poussins on individual heated plates and pass the sauce round separately.

FEUILLETÉ OF RABBIT WITH PEA PURÉE AND SORREL SAUCE

SERVES 4

225 g/8 oz puff pastry

PEA PURÉE:
100 g/4 oz shelled peas
15 g/½ oz onion, chopped finely
25 g/1 oz butter
6 tablespoons chicken stock
6 tablespoons single cream

RABBIT:
thigh and saddle of a 2 kg/4½ lb rabbit
100 g/4 oz butter
salt
freshly ground pepper

SORREL SAUCE:
4 tablespoons single cream
1 bunch sorrel (leaves only), chopped
  roughly
4 tablespoons beurre blanc (recipe follows)

TO COOK THE PASTRY: roll out the pastry on a floured board and cut it in 4 oblong pieces measuring 8.5 cm × 7 cm/3¼ × 2¾ inches. Bake in a preheated 200°C/400°F, Gas Mark 6 oven until it is well-risen and golden brown. Set aside.

TO MAKE THE PEA PURÉE: sauté the peas with onion and butter. Add the chicken stock and cream and reduce it until the peas are cooked and the liquid is absorbed. Purée in a blender or food processor and set aside in a warm place.

TO COOK THE RABBIT AND SAUCE: remove the bones from the rabbit and slice the meat thinly into 2 × 7 cm/¾ × 2¾ inch strips. Melt the butter in a non-stick pan and sauté the strips. Season with salt and pepper to taste. Remove them from the pan when only just cooked and keep warm. Add the cream to the pan, bring to the boil and add the sorrel leaves, then the beurre blanc. Heat the sauce but do not allow it to boil or the sauce will separate.

TO ASSEMBLE THE FEUILLETÉ: while you are cooking the rabbit, reheat the pastry in a preheated 160°C/325°F, Gas Mark 3 oven. Split the pastries and place the bases on 4 warmed plates. Spoon on the pea purée and arrange the rabbit on top. Place on the pastry lid and spoon sorrel sauce around the base. Serve at once.

VARIATION: for those who aren't fond of rabbit, or just for a change, this feuilleté could easily be made with pheasant or chicken, using the same method. Spinach leaves could be substituted for sorrel.

Rabbit and sorrel make a perfect partnership. Other ingredients that will enhance the flavour of rabbit are mustard, white wine, dry cider and thyme.

BEURRE BLANC

SERVES 4

2 tablespoons white wine vinegar
120 ml/4 fl oz white wine
2 shallots, chopped finely
1 tablespoon single cream
150 g/5 oz butter, cut in small pieces
salt
freshly ground pepper

Simmer the vinegar, wine and shallots slowly in a stainless steel saucepan until about 2 tablespoons of the liquid remains. Add the cream and return to the boil. Remove from the heat and, with a small wire whisk, beat in the butter, piece by piece. Season and serve at once.

THE GAME MENU

Of all available meats, wild game is the only one that is seasonal, and is always regarded as something special. Traditional accompaniments, however, may be too rich for modern tastes. Instead of game chips, consider tiny new potatoes boiled in their skins, and served with a sprinkling of lemon juice and finely chopped apple-mint. Alternatively, use brown rice or fragrant basmati rice to fill individual moulds that can be inverted on the plate. Line each oiled mould with blanched spinach or sorrel leaves before filling them with the cooked rice. For extra flavour, add a few chopped cèpes, prunes, juniper berries or capers.

Feuilleté of Rabbit with Pea Purée and Sorrel Sauce is an appropriate autumn dish

MEAT DISHES

RARE FILLET OF BEEF WITH MUSTARD BÉARNAISE SAUCE

When cooking for large numbers of people, choose dishes that can basically be prepared beforehand and put together quickly on the day. Here the beef may be cooked 1 day ahead of serving and refrigerated overnight.

SERVES 20

8 tablespoons mixed whole peppercorns (preferably white, green and black)
1 tablespoon ground cumin
3 × 1 kg/2 lb thick fillets of beef trimmed of all fat and membrane
2 tablespoons oil

MUSTARD BÉARNAISE SAUCE:
6 egg yolks
freshly ground black pepper
6 tablespoons tarragon vinegar
3 teaspoons dry mustard
2 tablespoons dry white wine
1 tablespoon redcurrant jelly
225 g/8 oz butter, cut in small pieces

TO SERVE:
fresh asparagus spears, lightly cooked

Crush the peppercorns using a pestle and mortar or a board and rolling pin. Mix them with the ground cumin. Coat the beef fillets in peppercorns. Heat the oil in a large frying pan or flameproof baking dish. Place the beef fillets in the pan and, over a fairly high heat, brown them on all sides. Keep turning them so that they will cook evenly. Cook in this manner for about 15 minutes. The meat will be rare and moist in the middle and crisp and tasty on the outside. Cool and set aside. If cooked the day before and refrigerated, take the fillets out in the morning, so that they will be at room temperature when served.

TO MAKE THE BÉARNAISE SAUCE: place the egg yolks in a stainless steel bowl and add the pepper, vinegar, mustard, wine and redcurrant jelly. Whisk together well. Place the bowl over a saucepan of simmering water, making sure the water is not touching the bottom of the bowl, and whisk until the mixture thickens. Gradually add the pieces of butter, whisking well. Remove the bowl from the heat, cover and set aside in a warm place. If the sauce curdles due to excessive heat, a tablespoon of iced water beaten in will restore it.

TO SERVE: slice the meat thinly and serve 3 slices per person with mustard béarnaise sauce. Serve with spears of fresh asparagus.

BEEF FILLET CARPACCIO WITH SAFFRON AND PARMESAN SLICES

SERVES 4

6 tablespoons olive oil
1 tablespoon lemon juice
few strands of saffron
2 sticks celery, sliced finely
1 artichoke heart, sliced finely
4 button mushrooms, sliced finely
salt
freshly ground black pepper
1 piece frozen fillet (tail end)
fresh piece of Parmesan cheese
1 × 50 g/2 oz tin anchovies, drained and cut in very thin strips
1 × 70 g/2½ oz jar capers, drained

ACCOMPANIMENTS:
mustard-flavoured vinaigrette

Heat the olive oil gently with the lemon juice and saffron strands. Cool, then add the celery, artichoke and mushrooms. Season with salt and pepper and leave for 2-4 hours for the flavours to infuse.

Take the fillet out of the freezer and let it stand for 5 minutes. Slice it as finely as possible, in about 2 mm/⅛ inch slices. Lay a single layer of beef on each plate. Surround it with marinated vegetables and finely sliced Parmesan cheese. Decorate trellis-fashion with the anchovies and halved capers and serve with a herbed mustard dressing.

STUFFED LOIN OF PORK WITH A ROSEMARY CRUST

SERVES 4-6

2 kg/4½ lb piece of pork loin, skin removed
12 fresh dates, stones removed

CRUST:
1 teaspoon salt
½ teaspoon ground peppercorns
1 bunch rosemary leaves, chopped finely
1 clove garlic, chopped
50 g/2 oz breadcrumbs
50 g/2 oz melted butter

SAUCE:
1 onion, peeled and chopped
1 tablespoon oil
2 tablespoons sherry
350 ml/12 fl oz chicken stock
100 g/4 oz butter, cut in cubes

GARNISH:
fresh dates
sprigs of rosemary

TO PREPARE THE ROAST: remove the bones and trim the loin. Make an incision right through the centre lengthways and fill it with dates.

TO MAKE THE CRUST: mix together the salt, peppercorns, half the rosemary, garlic and breadcrumbs and pat them thickly over the pork. Drizzle over the melted butter and roast in a preheated 180°C/350°F, Gas Mark 4 oven for 45 minutes or until the juice runs clear when the meat is pierced.

TO MAKE THE SAUCE: sauté the onion in the oil until it is cooked but not coloured. Add the sherry, the remaining rosemary and the chicken stock. Reduce the liquid by half and whisk in the butter cubes, one by one, making sure each has been incorporated before adding the next. Strain and keep hot.

TO SERVE: slice the pork. Pour a little sauce on each serving plate and arrange the pork slices on top. Garnish with fresh dates and a sprig of rosemary.

CÔTE DE BOEUF WITH AÏOLI

SERVES 6

AÏOLI WITH TOMATO:
5 egg yolks
3 cloves garlic, crushed
salt
freshly ground black pepper
2 tablespoons lemon juice
175 ml/6 fl oz olive oil
175 ml/6 fl oz peanut oil
2 tablespoons boiling water
2 tomatoes

STEAK:
6 rib steaks on the bone
salt and pepper
vegetable oil (optional)

TO MAKE THE AÏOLI: place the egg yolks, garlic, salt, pepper and lemon juice in a blender or food processor and process them. With the

Stuffed Loin of Pork with a Rosemary Crust uses fresh dates for a sweet contrast

motor running, gradually add the oils until the aïoli thickens. Mix in the boiling water. Skin and seed the tomatoes and cut them into small dice. Just before serving, add the tomatoes to the aïoli.

TO COOK THE STEAKS: the steaks can either be cooked under the grill, over the barbecue, or on a top plate or griller. Season the steaks with salt and pepper immediately before cooking. If you use a top plate or griller, brush the plate lightly with olive oil to prevent the steaks from sticking. Cook to taste and serve on a heated plate with the aïoli and rosti (recipe follows).

INDIVIDUAL ROSTI

SERVES 6

*6 medium potatoes, peeled and cut into
  wafer-thin slices
100 g/4 oz butter, melted
salt
freshly ground black pepper*

Butter 6 × 8 cm/3 inch tart tins. Place the
potato slices in layers seasoned with salt
and pepper, and pour a little melted butter
over the top. Press the potatoes firmly into
the tins. Cook in a preheated 200°C/400°F,
Gas Mark 6 oven on the centre shelf for 25
minutes, or until the rosti are cooked and
golden.

BOEUF À LA FICELLE

SERVES 6

*1 × 1.5 kg/3 lb fillet of beef
2 × 475 g/15 oz cans beef consommé
500 ml/18 fl oz water
salt
freshly ground pepper*

SAUCE:
*2 tablespoons single cream or more if
  necessary
3 teaspoons Dijon mustard
salt
freshly ground pepper*

Strip all fat and sinews from the fillet and
tie the meat with string to form a firm roll.
Bring the consommé and water to boil in a
large saucepan or fish kettle, add salt and
pepper and place the fillet in the boiling
stock. (The fillet must be covered with
liquid. Add more boiling water if necessary). Bring the stock back to the boil.

Boeuf à la Ficelle with Potatoes Janet

Remove the pan from the heat and allow it
to stand, covered, for 25 minutes. Place the
meat on the upturned lid. Cover with foil.
Leave it to rest for 15 minutes.
TO MAKE THE SAUCE: reduce the stock to
250 ml/8 fl oz, add the cream and bring it to
just below boiling point. Whip in the
mustard and season with salt and pepper.
TO SERVE: slice the beef thinly and place on
individual plates. Spoon over a little sauce.
Serve with Potatoes Janet (recipe follows).

POTATOES JANET

SERVES 6

*8 medium to large potatoes, peeled and
  sliced three-quarters of the way through
  at 1 cm/¹⁄₂ inch intervals
225 g/8 oz butter, melted
2 tablespoons dried rosemary
salt
freshly ground pepper*

In a dish pour the butter on the potatoes.
Add the rosemary, salt and pepper. Bake
for 1½ hours in a preheated 150°C/300°F,
Gas Mark 2 oven, basting frequently.

BOARDROOM FILLET

SERVES 6

*1 × 1 kg/2 lb fillet of beef
225 g/8 oz butter, melted
freshly ground pepper
sea salt
1 tablespoon boiling water*

Strip all membrane and fat from the fillet
with a sharp knife. Tie it with light twine at
just over 2.5 cm/1 inch intervals to keep the
fillet in a good shape. Preheat the oven to
220°C/425°F, Gas Mark 7. Place the fillet in
a roasting tin, pour the melted butter over
and sprinkle it with pepper and salt. Place
the tin on the centre shelf of the oven and
cook the beef for 5 minutes by a timer, to
seal the outside. Remove the meat from the
oven. Add the tablespoon of boiling water
to the butter around the meat and baste the
meat well.
   Return the tin to the oven and reduce
the temperature to 180°C/350°F, Gas Mark
4. Continue to cook the meat for a further
30 minutes, basting it 2 or 3 times during
cooking. Remove the meat from the oven
and allow it to cool on a wire rack.
   Serve the fillet, sliced, with béarnaise
sauce (recipe follows) and with a fresh
mixed salad.

BÉARNAISE SAUCE

SERVES 6

*5 tablespoons white wine vinegar
175 ml/6 fl oz white wine
a handful of parsley stems
1 onion, chopped
2 tablespoons dried tarragon
5 egg yolks
225 g/8 oz butter, cut in small pieces*

Place all the ingredients except the eggs and butter in a small stainless steel saucepan. Place over a low heat and simmer until the liquid is reduced to about 2 tablespoons. Strain the liquid, pressing down on any solids to extract their essence. Discard the solids. Return all of the essence to a clean saucepan, add the yolks and whisk well together. Stand the saucepan over very low heat and stir the mixture with a wooden spoon until it thickens a little. Quickly remove it from the heat and add a little butter. Return the pan to the heat and whisk in the pieces of butter, 2 or 3 at a time, until the sauce is emulsified. Pour the sauce into a bowl, cover and serve separately when cool.

STUFFED LETTUCE IN BROTH

SERVES 12

24 medium lettuce leaves – use darker
coloured leaves from about 3 heads of
lettuce
575 g/1¼ lb minced pork and veal
2 eggs
2 cloves garlic, crushed
1 tablespoon chopped parsley
1 teaspoon chopped fresh marjoram or
¼ teaspoon crumbled dry marjoram
salt
freshly ground pepper
freshly grated nutmeg
1 litre/1¾ pints rich stock (preferably veal)
well strained through muslin

GARNISH:
freshly grated Parmesan cheese

Wash the lettuce leaves carefully. Trim the tough ends and scrape the heavy ribs if necessary, making sure that the leaves are not torn or bruised. Blanch the leaves in

Boardroom Fillet served with Béarnaise Sauce makes an appetising lunch

batches of 2 or 3 in lightly salted boiling water for about 30-40 seconds. Drain them immediately and lie them flat in a single layer on a tea towel or paper towel.

Combine the pork and veal mince, eggs, garlic, parsley and marjoram with salt, pepper and nutmeg to taste; mix well. Place about 1 level tablespoon of the mixture in the centre of each leaf. Fold the bottom of the leaf over the filling, then fold in the sides. Roll them up tightly. Each

lettuce roll should fit in a soup spoon.

Arrange the rolls in a single layer in a shallow flameproof casserole. Add enough stock to just cover the lettuce rolls. Simmer, covered, for about 20 minutes over a medium-low heat. Heat the remaining stock separately and taste for seasoning.
TO SERVE: heat individual deep soup plates and place 2 rolls in each. Gently pour in the hot stock, sprinkle with grated Parmesan and serve at once.

71

FILLET STEAK WITH RAISINS, SERVED WITH MUSHROOM AND CARROT TIMBALES

SERVES 6

SAUCE:
1 medium onion, chopped finely
175 ml/6 fl oz red wine
sprig of thyme
1 teaspoon crushed black peppercorns
400 ml/14 fl oz thin demi-glace sauce (see
*   page 75)*
40 g/1½ oz raisins
salt
freshly ground pepper

TIMBALES:
1 large carrot
200 g/7 oz mushrooms
1 medium onion, chopped finely
1 sprig thyme
a little butter
300 ml/½ pint double cream
2 eggs
salt
freshly ground pepper

STEAK:
6 middle cuts of fillet, about 10 cm/
*   4 inches long and 5 cm/2 inches thick*
15 g/½ oz crushed black peppercorns
a little clarified butter (ghee)

TO MAKE THE SAUCE: place the onion in the pan with the wine, thyme and peppercorns. Reduce the liquid by half, add the demi-glace sauce and cook for 10 minutes. Strain the sauce, add the raisins and season with salt and pepper to taste. Keep hot.
TO MAKE THE TIMBALES: grease 6 small timbale moulds well. Carefully slice off long strips of carrot with a peeler, about 8 cm/3¼ inches wide. Cut enough strips of carrot to line all the moulds. Blanch the carrot strips in boiling water. Drain them and line the moulds with the strips.

Sauté the mushrooms, onion and thyme in a little butter. When the vegetables are cooked, purée them in a blender. Add the cream, eggs and seasoning. Pour the mushroom mixture into the lined moulds. Place them in a dish of water and bake in a preheated 180°C/350°F, Gas Mark 4 oven until the mixture is firm to the touch, about 20 minutes. Keep the timbales hot but do not let them overcook.
TO COOK THE STEAK: roll the pieces of steak in crushed peppercorns. Fry them until ready in a buttered pan or just seal them in the pan and finish the cooking in the oven.
TO SERVE: turn out the timbales on to individual serving plates. Slice each steak into 4 neat slices and arrange them on the plates. Spoon over the hot sauce and serve immediately.

VEAL ROLLS WITH LEMON MOUSSE SAUCE

SERVES 6

6 veal escalopes
freshly ground black pepper
1 bunch fresh young spinach
6 thin slices smoked salmon

LEMON MOUSSE SAUCE:
100 ml/3½ fl oz double cream
50 g/2 oz butter
juice of 1 lemon
pinch of salt
pinch of finely ground black pepper
200 ml/⅓ pint stiffly whipped cream

ACCOMPANIMENTS:
selection of summer vegetables, lightly
*   steamed*

Place the escalopes between sheets of greaseproof paper. Flatten them as thinly as possible with a mallet. Sprinkle the escalopes with the ground black pepper.

Wash and drain the spinach leaves. Lay them on the escalopes and place a slice of smoked salmon over the spinach. Roll the veal as tightly as possible and secure each roll with a toothpick. Bake in a preheated 180°C/350°F, Gas Mark 4 oven for approximately 20 minutes.
TO MAKE THE LEMON MOUSSE SAUCE: heat the double cream and butter together but do not let them boil. Add the lemon juice, salt and pepper. Just before serving, fold in the whipped cream.

TO SERVE: remove the veal rolls from the oven and serve them sliced, with the lemon mousse sauce and a selection of lightly steamed summer vegetables.

MARINATED CÔTE DE BOEUF

SERVES 6

MARINADE:
120 ml/4 fl oz pineapple juice
120 ml/4 fl oz cup soy sauce
2 tablespoons chopped fresh ginger
4 tablespoons sherry
1 tablespoon butter
1 teaspoon dry mustard
1 teaspoon chopped garlic
½ teaspoon curry powder

MEAT:
rib roast of beef containing 6 ribs, trimmed
*   well by the butcher*
melted butter

ACCOMPANIMENTS:
boiled baby potatoes
melted butter
green salad

Combine all the ingredients for the marinade. Place the meat in a close-fitting glass or china dish and pour over the marinade. Let the meat marinate in the refrigerator for 12-24 hours, turning it over from time to time. Remove from the refrigerator and allow to stand until the meat reaches room temperature before cooking it. The meat can be cooked in the oven or in a covered barbecue.

TO COOK IN THE OVEN: place the meat on a rack in a baking dish and pour over some melted butter. Cook on the centre shelf of a preheated 190°C/375°F, Gas Mark 5 oven for 1-1¼ hours. Let the meat rest for 20 minutes before carving. This will make carving much easier and give you a clean slice.

TO BARBECUE: cook the meat in a covered barbecue as instructed by the manufacturer and allow to rest for 20 minutes before serving.

TO SERVE: cut the beef in 6 slices and serve with buttered, boiled baby potatoes and a tossed green salad.

ROASTING BEEF

Fillet of beef is excellent for roasting. It has little or no fat, which makes it an attractive cut for those who prefer lean meat. It is also the most tender of cuts. The best way to roast meat is to put it into a hot oven (230°C/450°F, Gas Mark 8) for 20 minutes to seal the outside. Then reduce the heat and cook slowly (at about 150°C/300°F, Gas Mark 2) for the remaining cooking time. This makes the meat more tender.

Choose Veal Rolls with Lemon Mousse Sauce for a delicately flavoured main course

NOISETTES OF LAMB SERVED ON ONION SOUBISE WITH MELTING MINT BUTTER

SERVES 6

MINT BUTTER:
225 g/8 oz butter, softened
3 tablespoons finely chopped fresh mint
juice of ½ lemon
freshly ground pepper

ONION SOUBISE:
3 large onions, peeled
salt
25 g/1 oz butter
15 g/½ oz plain flour
175 ml/6 fl oz hot milk
pinch of grated nutmeg
freshly ground pepper

NOISETTES:
25 g/1 oz butter
1 tablespoon oil
6 lamb noisettes

ACCOMPANIMENT:
selection of crisp green vegetables

TO MAKE THE MINT BUTTER: blend all the ingredients in a blender or food processor and blend for a few minutes. Form the butter into a roll. Wrap it in cling film and refrigerate until serving time.

TO MAKE THE ONION SOUBISE: cook the whole onions in salted water until they are quite tender. Drain them and set them aside. Melt the butter in a small saucepan. Add the flour and cook for 1 minute. Pour on the hot milk and whisk the sauce until it is thick and free from lumps. Season with nutmeg, salt and pepper to taste. Place the onions with the sauce in a blender or food processor and purée until the sauce is smooth.

Use a light touch in the arrangement of Rack of Lamb Stuffed with Courgettes

TO COOK THE NOISETTES: melt the butter and oil in a frying pan. When the mixture is very hot, put in the noisettes and cook them for about 8 minutes each side, turning frequently to prevent burning.

TO SERVE: place a portion of the hot onion soubise on six individual heated plates. Place a noisette of lamb on each plate, top with a slice of mint butter and serve at once with vegetables of your choice.

RACK OF LAMB STUFFED WITH COURGETTES

SERVES 1

1 × 3 chop rack of lamb
1 baby green courgette
6 carrot batons
8 green and yellow courgette batons
a knob of butter
salt
freshly ground pepper
4 tablespoons lamb jus (lamb gravy made from bones, chopped vegetables or mirepoix, water and wine, reduced and thickened with a little cornflour or arrowroot)
2 courgette blossoms, cut in strips
1 carrot fan (optional)

Using a round steel make a tunnel through the eye of the meat of the rack of lamb. Blanch the baby green courgette and refresh in cold water. Push it carefully into the hole through the lamb. Roast the rack in a preheated 200°C/400°F, Gas Mark 6 oven for approximately 15 minutes. Remove it from the oven and rest it in a warm place for 10 minutes.

Meanwhile, blanch the vegetable batons and toss them in the butter. Season with salt and pepper. Heat the lamb gravy and add the strips of courgette flowers. Cut the rack into 3 cutlets and arrange on a warm plate. Surround the cutlets with batons of vegetables and sauce. If desired, garnish with a carrot fan and serve immediately.
TO MAKE A CARROT FAN: cut a carrot in 4 lengthways and then cut a small melon-shaped wedge from one of the lengths. With a sharp knife, cut from the wide edge of the wedge to the thin edge, but do not cut it right through. Keep the wedge in one piece. Press down on the carrot with the palm of the hand to shape.

DEBONED LOIN OF LAMB WITH PORT WINE SAUCE

SERVES 6

6 pieces lamb mignon, cut from the saddle, each weighing 150 g/5 oz
50 g/2 oz butter
15 g/½ oz shallots, chopped finely
4 tablespoons red wine
6 tablespoons demi-glace sauce (recipe follows)
150 ml/¼ pint single cream
salt
freshly ground pepper
dash of port

Trim the lamb and remove all the fat. Heat half the butter in a pan, sauté the lamb and seal it on all sides. Place it in a preheated 180°C/350°F, Gas Mark 4 oven to finish cooking. When the lamb is cooked but still pink inside, remove it from the oven and leave it to rest.
TO MAKE THE SAUCE: drain the fat from the pan and add the shallots, red wine and demi-glace sauce to the pan. Reduce by one-third. Add the cream, bring the sauce to the boil, then beat in the remaining butter. Season with salt and pepper and add port to taste. Strain the sauce and keep it hot, but do not let it boil.
TO SERVE: slice the lamb. Pour the sauce on to 6 heated serving plates and arrange slices of lamb on top.

DEMI-GLACE SAUCE

MAKES 1 LITRE/1¾ PINTS

2 kg/4½ lb veal neck bones
1 large veal shank, cut in sections
2 pig's trotters
2 onions, chopped
4 carrots, sliced
1 stick celery, sliced
1 whole bulb garlic, peeled and broken up
6-8 sprigs thyme
2 bay leaves
3 tablespoons tomato purée
1 litre/1¾ pints wine, white or red

Spread the veal bones, veal shanks and trotters in a large roasting tin and roast in a preheated 200°C/400°F, Gas Mark 6 oven for 2 hours until they are crispy and golden. Turn the bones a few times so that they brown on all sides.

Pour off all the fat. Add the onions, carrots, celery, peeled garlic cloves, thyme, bay leaves and tomato purée to the tin and mix them around well. Pour in the wine. Reduce the oven temperature to 160°C/325°F, Gas Mark 3 and cook the meat until it resembles a brown oven stew. Transfer the braised bones and juices to a large saucepan. Pour enough water into the roasting tin to help scrape up all the residue left in the tin. Pour the mixture into the pan with the bones and fill it to within 5 cm/2 inches of the top with cold water. Bring it to the boil and skim off the grease from the top as the stock cooks.

Cover the pan, lower the heat and leave it to simmer for 12 hours. Strain off the stock into a clean pan and leave it to cool. When the fat has set, remove and discard it. Put the cleaned stock back into the pot and reduce it to half the amount. Strain through a fine strainer.

PAILLARD OF LAMB VINAIGRETTE

SERVES 4

*2 lamb rib-eyes, cleaned and trimmed of
all fat and membrane*

MARINADE:
*120 ml/4 fl oz olive oil
120 ml/4 fl oz white wine
1 bay leaf
1 onion, chopped finely
1 carrot, chopped finely
freshly ground black pepper*

VINAIGRETTE:
*120 ml/4 fl oz vinegar
250 ml/8 fl oz olive oil
salt
freshly ground black pepper
1 clove garlic, peeled and crushed
1 teaspoon prepared English mustard
1 teaspoon chopped mint
fresh cream*

Cut the rib-eyes lengthways, ¾ of the way
through, using a sharp knife. Open the
meat up and flatten it with a mallet. Do not
make the meat too thin. Cut into serving-
sized slices and set aside.

Mix together all the ingredients for the
marinade and marinate the pieces of lamb
for 6-8 hours.

Remove the lamb from the marinade
and char-grill it, but do not overcook it as
the lamb will dry. Heat all the ingredients
for the vinaigrette except the mint and
cream very slowly, but do not allow them
to boil. Remove from the heat and add the
mint and a little fresh cream.

TO SERVE: place the slices of meat on
individual serving plates and pour over a
little heated vinaigrette. Serve at once with
steamed baby carrots and turnips and
boiled new potatoes.

LAMB RIB-EYE FLEUR-DE-LIS

SERVES 4

2 lamb rib-eyes, cut from the loin

MARINADE:
*sprigs of rosemary and lemon thyme,
chopped roughly
1 large clove garlic
2 bay leaves
1 lemon, squeezed and quartered
175 ml/6 fl oz red wine
175 ml/6 fl oz crème de cassis
2 tablespoons olive oil
salt
freshly ground black pepper*

DEMI-GLACE SAUCE:
*lamb bones or a piece of lamb neck
1 onion, chopped
1 carrot, chopped
1 stick celery, chopped
2 tablespoons oil
marinade mixture
1 teaspoon tomato purée
crème de cassis to taste
a little arrowroot*

GARNISH:
*thin slices of apple, sautéed in butter, or
clusters of blackcurrants
sprigs of rosemary*

Mix all the marinade ingredients together.
Prick the rib-eyes a few times with a sharp
knife and marinate overnight, or for at least
3 hours, in the refrigerator, turning them
over once or twice.

TO MAKE THE SAUCE: brown the lamb bones,
chopped onion, carrot and celery in the oil
until brown but not burned.

Remove the lamb from the marinade
and set it aside. Pour the liquid from the
marinade over the bones and add water to
cover. Stir in the tomato purée. Cover the
saucepan and simmer the sauce for about
45 minutes. Remove the lid and boil the
mixture rapidly until it is reduced by
two-thirds. Strain the liquid, discard the
solids and skim the fat from the surface. Add
the crème de cassis to taste and a little
arrowroot, dissolved in water, to thicken.

TO COOK THE LAMB: pat the rib-eyes dry
with paper towels and either barbecue or
grill them for about 5 minutes on each
side, if you like pink lamb.

Slice the lamb very thinly and arrange
on the demi-glace sauce. Garnish with
apple slices or blackcurrants, and rosemary sprigs.

VEGETABLES

Lamb is best served with a mélange of
vegetables cut in small pieces and
steamed quickly, then tossed in butter
and black pepper. Choose vegetables for
their colour, texture and shape; tiny baby
beetroots should be steamed separately
and added to the other vegetables at the
last minute, otherwise all the vegetables
will be pink.

Radishes, red peppers, asparagus,
pumpkin, green beans, yellow beans,
sweet potatoes, baby carrots, spring
onions and even some slivers of fresh
ginger can be used in any combination.

*For a particularly special dinner dish,
Lamb Rib-Eye Fleur-de-Lis is a
spectacular choice*

DESSERTS

A flourish for the end of the meal:
some great ideas that are a natural conclusion

The end of the meal calls for something that will give a feeling of satisfaction, but not satiation. Puddings may be as simple or as sophisticated as you like. Plainest of all, but no less delicious if it is presented with style, is a bowl of fresh seasonal fruits. The perfection of fresh fruit lends itself to one-colour arrangements – such as all red berries or a green selection of grapes, apples and kiwifruit – as well as to an assortment of contrasting colours.

The options for using fruit in some way to complete the meal are endless. Superbly fresh-tasting desserts range from the simplicity of a slice of Watermelon with Lemon Cheese to the impressive appeal of individual hot Orange Soufflés. The tang of citrus can be appreciated best, perhaps, in iced desserts such as a lime or orange sorbet, as welcome at the end of the meal as when served between courses.

A cheese platter as a conclusion is a natural solution to the problem of a fine, suitable finale. Served with fruit such as grapes, fresh berries or the new season's crisp autumn apples, there can be almost nothing to improve on it. Other refreshingly simple ideas are figs served with a little mascarpone, pears with slices of Parmesan cheese, and goats' cheese dressed with vinaigrette and sprinkled with fresh garden herbs.

At the end of the meal, presentation is extremely important. The prettiest china, most brilliant crystal or most creative pottery will enhance food and ensure that your meal leaves a lasting impression of natural style.

At the end of a meal based on fresh and natural foods, the palate will delight in such innovative combinations as Pears and Parmesan; what is sweet, juicy and aromatic is accentuated by its sharp and salty partner. Finding the fruit that's right for the cheese is one of the rewards of fresh menu-making

SORBET

The following fruits may be used for the sorbets: apple, pineapple, lime, blueberry, raspberry, passionfruit, strawberry, tangerine, kiwifruit, pink grapefruit, pomegranate, orange, blackcurrant or redcurrant.

SERVES 4

500 ml/18 fl oz fruit purée or juice of fruit

SIMPLE SYRUP:
150 g/5 oz sugar
500 ml/18 fl oz water

ACCOMPANIMENT:
a selection of light biscuits

Pass the fruit purée through a sieve to remove seeds or pulp.

TO MAKE THE SYRUP: mix the sugar and water together in a saucepan. Bring to the boil and stir until the sugar is dissolved. Remove the pan from the heat and leave to cool.

Blend the simple syrup and purée together. Place the mixture in an ice-cream maker and freeze.

Serve a combination of flavours and colours on each plate, with biscuits.

SUGAR QUANTITIES

Less sugar can be used in these recipes, according to taste. In sorbets, reduce the amount of sugar and water for the syrup proportionately, and add more of the fruit purée (unless the fruit is sharp).

Present your guests with a range of sorbets to refresh them after a fine meal

CANTALOUPE MOUSSELINE WITH RHUBARB ICE-CREAM

SERVES 6

CANTALOUPE MOUSSELINE:
100 g/4 oz sugar
2 tablespoons water
3 egg yolks
2 teaspoons gelatine
200 ml/⅓ pint cantaloupe or orange juice
200 ml/⅓ pint double cream, whipped
3 egg whites, beaten to stiff peaks

RHUBARB ICE-CREAM:
1 bunch rhubarb
275 g/10 oz sugar
juice of 1 lemon
6 egg yolks
150 g/5 oz sugar
350 ml/12 fl oz milk
200 ml/⅓ pint double cream, whipped

TO DECORATE:
thin slices of cantaloupe melon

TO MAKE THE CANTALOUPE MOUSSELINE: bring the sugar and water to the boil and set aside to cool. Pour it on to the egg yolks, whisking constantly. Continue to whisk, with the bowl set over boiling water, until the mixture is thick.

Soften the gelatine in the cold water for 1 minute, melt over boiling water and add to the egg yolk mixture. Stir well. Leave to cool. When the mixture is cold, set the bowl over crushed ice and whisk in the fruit juice. Whisk until the mixture is thick. Fold in the whipped cream and beaten egg white.

Rinse 6 × 250 ml/8 fl oz moulds with cold water and pour in the mousseline. Cover and refrigerate for at least 6 hours.
TO MAKE THE RHUBARB ICE-CREAM: wash the rhubarb and cut in pieces. Place in a saucepan with the sugar and lemon juice.

Cook slowly for about 30 minutes. Push the rhubarb through a sieve and set it aside.

Mix the egg yolks with the sugar. Bring the milk to the boil and pour on to the egg yolks. Return the mixture to the saucepan and cook over a low heat, stirring constantly, until it coats the back of a spoon. Do not boil. Leave to cool. Fold in the cream and rhubarb purée and freeze the mixture in an ice-cream maker.
TO SERVE: turn each mousseline out on to a chilled plate. Place 2 scoops of rhubarb ice-cream next to the mousseline and garnish with slices of fresh cantaloupe.

LA SOUPE FROIDE DE MELON À LA CANNELLE
(CHILLED MELON SOUP FLAVOURED WITH CINNAMON)

SERVES 8

2 cantaloupes (total weight 1.5 kg/3 lb)
225 g/8 oz sugar
250 ml/8 fl oz water
juice of ½ lemon or to taste
ground cinnamon to taste

TO DECORATE:
strawberry ice-cream (see page 82)
mango ice-cream (see page 84)
strawberries, cut in half
sprigs of mint

Peel and seed the melon and purée it in a blender. Make a syrup by bringing the sugar and water to the boil and set it aside to cool. Mix the melon purée, sugar syrup, lemon juice and cinnamon together. Cover and refrigerate.
TO SERVE: serve the soup in chilled wide soup bowls with a small scoop each of strawberry ice-cream and mango ice-cream. Garnish with halved strawberries and sprigs of mint. Serve immediately.

LA COUPE NINOSHKA

SERVES 4

6 medium peaches
blackcurrant syrup

SORBETS:
350 g/12 oz sugar
500 ml/18 fl oz water
500 ml/18 fl oz pink grapefruit juice
500 ml/18 fl oz lemon juice
chilled vodka

Peel the peaches by immersing them in boiling water for a few seconds. Cut the flesh into 2 cm/¾ inch dice. Macerate in enough blackcurrant syrup to just cover them for at least 2 hours.
TO MAKE THE SORBETS: make a sugar syrup by boiling the sugar with the water for 5 minutes. Leave to cool.
TO MAKE THE PINK GRAPEFRUIT SORBET: mix the grapefruit juice with 250 ml/8 fl oz of sugar syrup. (If pink grapefruit are not available, add a few drops of grenadine to the grapefruit juice to colour it pink.)
TO MAKE THE LEMON SORBET: mix the lemon juice with 250 ml/8 fl oz sugar syrup. Churn both these mixtures separately in a sorbetière and place them, covered, in the freezer.
TO SERVE: drain the peach dice and divide them between 4 coupe glasses. Place a scoop of each sorbet on the peaches. At the table, drizzle about 2 teaspoons of ice-cold vodka over the sorbets.

STRAWBERRY ICE-CREAM

SERVES 4

225 g/8 oz strawberries
3 egg yolks
100 g/4 oz sugar, or a little more if the strawberries are not fully ripe
450 ml/³/4 pint single cream
¹/2 teaspoon lemon juice

Hull the strawberries and purée them in a blender or food processor. Beat the egg yolks with the sugar. Bring the cream to just below boiling point and pour it on to the egg mixture. Return the cream to the saucepan and stir it constantly over a low heat until the mixture thickens and coats the back of a wooden spoon. Do not allow to boil. Add the strawberry purée and lemon juice. Strain the strawberry custard and set it aside to cool. When the custard is completely cold, chill it in the refrigerator for 2-3 hours. Freeze it in an ice-cream maker. Store the ice-cream in a covered container in the freezer.

BISCUITS FOR ICES

Light, crisp biscuits or wafers provide an essential contrast to the texture of ice-creams and sorbets. There are innumerable shapes and textures to choose from – crunchy tuiles, fan-shaped wafers, tiny cornets – subtly flavoured with chocolate chips, coffee or spices. Few bought varieties of biscuit can match the taste of home-made ones.

PEACH MELBA REVISITED

SERVES 6

VANILLA ICE-CREAM:
500 ml/18 fl oz milk
1 vanilla pod, split lengthways
225 g/8 oz sugar
6 egg yolks
250 ml/8 fl oz double cream, lightly whipped

WAFERS:
100 g/4 oz unsalted butter
200 g/7 oz icing sugar
5¹/2 egg whites
150 g/5 oz plain flour, sifted
few drops vanilla essence

PEACHES:
500 ml/18 fl oz sugar
225 g/8 oz water
6 whole peaches

RASPBERRY COULIS:
450 g/1 lb raspberries (reserve a few good ones for garnish)
2 tablespoons caster sugar

TO SERVE:
200 ml/¹/3 pint double cream, lightly whipped
reserved whole raspberries
vanilla ice-cream
wafers
sprigs of mint

TO MAKE THE ICE-CREAM: bring the milk and vanilla pod to the boil with half the sugar. Beat the egg yolks with the remaining sugar. Pour the milk on to the egg mixture and whisk it well. Return the mixture to the pan and stir it over a low heat until the mixture thickens and coats the back of a spoon. Do not boil. Strain, allow to cool and fold in the cream. Chill in the refrigerator and freeze in an ice-cream maker.

TO MAKE THE WAFERS: beat the butter and icing sugar together until the mixture is white and fluffy. Still beating, gradually add the egg whites, then the flour and vanilla. Spoon or pipe very small rounds on to a buttered baking tray and bake in a pre-heated 230°C/450°F, Gas Mark 8 oven. The wafers are cooked when they turn brown around the edges. Quickly lift the wafers off the tin and pinch one side together to form a case. Leave them to cool on a cake rack.

TO PREPARE THE PEACHES: make a sugar syrup, bringing the sugar and water to the boil and stirring until the sugar is dissolved. Pour the syrup over the peaches and leave them to stand until they are cold.

TO MAKE THE RASPBERRY COULIS: place the raspberries and sugar in a blender or food processor and process until well puréed. Strain the purée and discard the seeds.

TO SERVE: carefully skin the peaches and remove the peach stones with a sharp knife or very small teaspoon, keeping the peaches whole. Add 2 tablespoons of raspberry coulis to the whipped cream and pipe the cream mixture into the centre of the peaches. Place the peaches in the centre of 6 chilled serving plates and encircle with whole raspberries. Spoon the raspberry coulis to one side of each peach, add a drop of cream to each pool of coulis and draw a skewer through to create a web effect. Pipe softened vanilla ice-cream into the wafer cases and arrange them to one side of the peaches. Decorate the top of the each peach with a sprig of mint and serve at once.

Pay your favoured guests the compliment of an elaborate fruit-based dessert like Peach Melba Revisited

FRESH MANGO ICE-CREAM

SERVES 4

4 egg yolks
150 g/5 oz sugar
250 ml/8 fl oz single cream
vanilla essence
300 ml/¹/₂ pint double cream, lightly
  whipped
3 or 4 fresh mangoes

Beat the egg yolks and sugar together.
Bring the single cream to just below
boiling point, pour it on to the egg mixture
and mix well. Return the mixture to the
saucepan and stir it constantly over a low
heat until the mixture thickens and coats
the back of a wooden spoon. Add the
vanilla essence and set the custard aside to
cool. When cold, fold in the whipped
cream.

   Peal the mangoes and purée the flesh in
a blender or food processor. Add the
purée to the custard mixture and mix well.
Chill it in the refrigerator for 2-3 hours,
then freeze in an ice-cream maker.

WATERMELON WITH LEMON CHEESE

SERVES 8

2 kg/4¹/₂ lb watermelon
225 g/8 oz ricotta cheese
grated rind and juice of 1 lemon
icing sugar

Peel and seed the watermelon and cut it in
cubes. Place in a covered bowl in the
refrigerator.

   Mix the ricotta cheese with the rind and
juice of the lemon in a bowl and beat with
a fork. Add icing sugar to taste and more

lemon juice if necessary. A sharp, lemon
taste is required as the cheese is too bland
to serve alone with watermelon. Serve the
cold watermelon in small chilled bowls
with spoonfuls of lemon cheese on top.

ORANGE AND GINGER SALAD

SERVES 6

6 navel oranges

SYRUP:
250 ml/8 fl oz water
225 g/8 oz sugar
3 tablespoons fine julienne of fresh ginger

TO SERVE:
whipped cream

Peel the oranges, slice them thinly and
spread the slices out on a large china dish.
Set them aside.
TO MAKE THE SYRUP: bring the water and sugar
to the boil and cook for 2 or 3 minutes.
Remove the pan from the heat and add the
ginger. Leave the syrup to cool and pour it
over the prepared oranges. Cover the dish
and refrigerate overnight. Serve with cream.

FRESH AND FRUITFUL

A fruity dessert is often the most refreshing of all. Fruit syrups and flan cases
can be prepared in advance, giving you
time to make an artistic masterpiece of
the final presentation.

RASPBERRY MASCARPONE CREAM

SERVES 6

450 g/1 lb sweet mascarpone, chilled
100 g/4 oz caster sugar
4 eggs, separated
4 tablespoons Italian liqueur (Nocello,
  Peach Leaf, Galliano) or marsala
225 g/8 oz fresh raspberries

ACCOMPANIMENT:
pine nut biscuits (recipe follows)

Whip the mascarpone, sugar and egg yolks
together until thick and creamy. Stir in the
liqueur or marsala. Beat the egg whites
until they hold stiff peaks and gently fold
them into the mascarpone mixture. Spoon
the mixture into individual bowls or
coupes. Scatter over the raspberries and
serve within 1 hour, with the biscuits.

PINE NUT BISCUITS

75 g/3 oz ground almonds
200 g/7 oz caster sugar
2 egg whites
pinch of salt
¹/₄ teaspoon vanilla essence
150 g/5 oz toasted pine nuts, chopped

Mix the almonds with half the sugar. Beat
the egg whites with salt until they hold soft
peaks. Gradually beat in the remaining
sugar and the vanilla essence. Fold the egg
whites into the almond/sugar mixture.

   Spread the pine nuts on to a baking
sheet. Drop in small pieces of the biscuit
mixture and lightly roll them in the pine
nuts. Bake the pieces on the centre shelf of
a preheated 190°C/375°F, Gas Mark 5 oven
for 15 minutes until golden. Store in an
airtight container.

BANANAS WITH MANGO COCONUT SAUCE

SERVES 6

12 bananas

SAUCE:
2 mangoes, puréed
500 ml/18 fl oz coconut milk (see page 38)
175 g/6 oz brown sugar
2 tablespoons lime juice

Gently heat the mango purée, coconut milk and brown sugar together. When the sugar has dissolved, leave the mixture to cool. Stir in the lime juice.

Barbecue the bananas on the lowest flame or over dying embers until they begin to caramelise. Pour the sauce on to individual serving plates and place 2 bananas on each. Serve immediately.

FRESH FRUITS WITH HOT SABAYON

SERVES 8

SABAYON:
12 egg yolks, well beaten
1 litre/1¾ pints dessert wine of your choice
2 tablespoons caster sugar (more if the
*   wine is not sweet enough)*

FRUIT:
slices of apple, pears, pineapple, oranges,
*   bananas, grapes, strawberries, kiwifruit*

Place all the ingredients for the sabayon in a large china or metal bowl standing over a pot of simmering water. Whisk until the sauce thickens. Pour it immediately into 8 soup plates and arrange the fruit on top.

Serve Bananas with Mango Coconut Sauce with cool grapes and whole mangoes

INDIVIDUAL PEAR OR RASPBERRY TARTS

MAKES 8 TARTS

PASTRY:
150 g/5 oz unsalted butter, softened
65 g/2¹/₂ oz caster sugar
40 g/1¹/₂ oz toasted hazelnuts, peeled and
  ground
1 egg, beaten
1 tablespoon water
pinch of salt
225 g/8 oz plain flour, sifted

FILLING:
5 eggs, beaten
150 g/5 oz sugar
1 heaped tablespoon rice flour
350 ml/12 fl oz double cream
3¹/₂ tablespoons Kirsch or pear liqueur
450 g/1 lb raspberries or 4 large poached
  pears, sliced

TO MAKE THE PASTRY: cream the butter and sugar together and add the ground hazelnuts. Add the beaten egg, water and salt and mix well. Add the sifted flour and mix it in lightly. Wrap the pastry in cling film and refrigerate it for at least 1 hour.

TO MAKE THE FILLING: whisk the eggs, sugar, rice flour, cream and the liqueur of your choice for a few minutes, until the mixture thickens slightly.

TO ASSEMBLE AND COOK THE TARTS: roll out the pastry and line 8 × 8 cm/3¹/₄ inch tart tins. Prick the bases with a fork and bake them in a preheated 200°C/400°F, Gas Mark 6 oven for 12 minutes or until they are golden. Arrange a layer of raspberries or pears in the tarts. Fill them with the cream mixture and bake in a preheated 190°C/375°F, Gas Mark 5 oven for 5 minutes or until the filling is set and each tart is golden brown on top.

STRAWBERRY SABLÉS

SERVES 10

PASTRY:
400 g/14 oz butter
200 g/7 oz sugar
6 egg yolks
1.25 kg/2¹/₂ lb plain flour, sifted

STRAWBERRY COULIS:
450 g/1 lb strawberries
250 ml/8 fl oz sugar syrup (225 g/8 oz
  sugar to 250 ml/8 fl oz water)
lemon juice

THE STRAWBERRIES:
1 kg/2 lb strawberries, hulled and cut in
  halves or quarters

TO DECORATE:
sifted icing sugar
10 perfect whole strawberries

TO MAKE THE SABLÉS: cream the butter and sugar together. Slowly beat in the egg yolks, being careful not to curdle the mixture. Add the flour all at once and mix together for a few minutes to form a smooth paste. Do not overmix as the pastry will crack. Place in the refrigerator wrapped in cling film, for 20 minutes or more.

Roll out on a floured board to about 3 mm/¹/₈ inch thick and, using an 8 cm/3¹/₄ inch fluted cutter, cut out 30 rounds. Place the rounds on a lightly greased baking sheet and prick the pastry with a fork. Bake in a preheated 180°C/350°F, Gas Mark 4 oven for 8-12 minutes until they are a light golden brown. Remove from the oven and cool on a rack. Store in an airtight container.

TO MAKE THE COULIS: blend the strawberries with the sugar syrup and process to make a purée. Add lemon juice to taste. Strain the purée and discard the seeds.

TO ASSEMBLE: place a pastry disc on each serving plate and cover it with cut strawberries. Place a second disc on top of the strawberries and cover again with cut strawberries. Place a third disc on top and dust with sifted icing sugar. Place a whole perfect strawberry on top of each sablé. Pour strawberry coulis around each sablé and serve immediately.

ORANGE SOUFFLÉS

SERVES 6

200 ml/¹/₃ pint milk
25 g/1 oz plain flour
65 g/2¹/₂ oz sugar
2 teaspoons butter
6 egg yolks, beaten
grated rind of 3 oranges
orange liqueur, to taste
9 egg whites

TO PREPARE SOUFFLÉ DISHES:
butter
caster sugar

In a saucepan, stir a little milk into the flour until the mixture is smooth. Whisk in the remaining milk and sugar. Place the pan over a low heat and cook slowly, stirring constantly until the mixture thickens. Remove from the heat and stir in the butter and beaten egg yolks. Flavour with grated orange rind and orange liqueur.

Beat the egg whites until they form soft peaks. Stir one quarter of the egg white into the sauce then gently fold in the remainder. Spoon the mixture into 6 × 250 ml/8 fl oz buttered soufflé dishes that have been dusted with caster sugar. Cook in a preheated 220°C/425°F, Gas Mark 7 oven for 12 minutes or till the soufflés are risen and golden. Serve at once.

Summery Orange Soufflés make a delicious alternative to the more familiar lemon version

Strawberries and Cream in Crisp Pastry Punnets provide an elegant finish

STRAWBERRIES AND CREAM IN CRISP PASTRY PUNNETS

SERVES 6

Prepare the pastry 1 day in advance.

SWEET PASTRY MIXTURE:
2 egg whites
100 g/4 oz plain flour
75 g/3 oz icing sugar
50 g/2 oz caster sugar
2 tablespoons double cream
vegetable oil

RASPBERRY COULIS:
450 g/1 lb fresh raspberries
250 ml/8 fl oz sugar syrup (see Strawberry
  Sablés, page 86)
120 ml/4 fl oz raspberry liqueur
  (Framboise)

TO FILL PUNNETS:
strawberries, hulled

TO DECORATE:
wild strawberry leaves
melted chocolate (optional)

TO MAKE THE PASTRY: lightly beat the egg whites and gradually add all the other ingredients except the vegetable oil until they are well combined. Beat in the cream last. Refrigerate in an airtight container overnight.

Cut templates to the shape of your choice from the lid of a plastic ice-cream container. Strips and circles were used for the ones illustrated here. Circles were cut to size from the bottom of a small jar and strips 7.5 cm/3 inches wide × the length of the jar's circumference. Brush a baking sheet with vegetable oil. Spread the templates with the pastry mixture, trim the edges and place them pastry-side down on the baking sheet. Peel off the templates carefully, leaving the pastry shapes on the tray. Cook only 2 pieces at a time on 1 sheet. Bake on the centre shelf of a preheated 190°C/375°F, Gas Mark 5 oven for 5-6 minutes until the pastry is light brown around the edges. Remove the sheet from the oven and, using a spatula, carefully but quickly remove the pastry and wrap strips around the small jar. The pastry is soft for only a short time so you have to work quickly. Store in an airtight tin immediately.

TO MAKE THE RASPBERRY COULIS: place all the ingredients in a blender or food processor and purée. Strain, discard the seeds and keep refrigerated in an airtight container:

TO SERVE: assemble the pastry punnets on individual plates. Place a circle of pastry on the plate with the punnet shape on top. Fill each one with strawberries and pour over the raspberry coulis. Garnish with wild strawberry leaves. If you are using chocolate, decorate the punnets before filling them: first pipe fine lines around the punnets and allow to harden. Then spread chocolate on the circles and place a punnet shape on top. Allow the chocolate to set before filling with strawberries.

POACHED PEARS WITH PASSIONFRUIT SYRUP

SERVES 6

1 litre/1¾ pints white wine
560 ml/20 fl oz water
300 g/10 oz sugar
rind of 1 lemon
6 firm pears
12 passionfruit, or enough to yield
  250 ml/8 fl oz juice

TO SERVE:
whipped cream

TO POACH THE PEARS: make a poaching syrup by boiling together the wine, 500 ml/18 fl oz of the water, 200 g/7 oz of the sugar and the lemon rind. Leave it to cool. Peel, halve and core the pears. Place them immediately into the syrup (the acid of the wine will stop the pears from discolouring). Bring the syrup to the boil, lower the heat and poach the pears gently for about 5 minutes, depending on how ripe they are. Leave the pears to cool in the syrup.

TO MAKE THE PASSIONFRUIT SYRUP: pass the pulp of the passionfruit through a fine sieve to yield 250 ml/8 fl oz juice. Combine the juice with the remaining water and sugar and bring it to the boil. As the syrup boils, the residual pulp will form a scum. Carefully skim this off as it forms, and reduce the liquid to about half its volume. The passionfruit syrup should be clear.

TO SERVE THE PEARS: lift the pears out of the syrup with a slotted spoon and place 2 halves on each of 6 serving plates. Starting at the bottom, cut each pear half into 10 or 12 slices, taking care not to slice through the top of the pear. Correctly cut, the pears need only be flattened with the fingers to fan out. Dribble a tablespoon of passionfruit syrup over each half and serve with whipped cream.

LAST – BUT NOT LEAST

A pause before serving the dessert is often appreciated by both your guests and yourself – and will add to the dramatic effect of a well-prepared and beautifully presented final dish.

BRANDY CORNET OF BERRIES

SERVES 6-8

2 tablespoons maple syrup
50 g/2 oz caster sugar
50 g/2 oz unsalted butter
50 g/2 oz plain flour, sifted
1 tablespoon powdered ginger
1 tablespoon brandy
1 teaspoon lemon juice

CRÈME ANGLAISE:
500 ml/18 fl oz milk
4 egg yolks
100 g/4 oz caster sugar
few drops vanilla essence

RASPBERRRY PURÉE
100 g/4 oz raspberries
1 tablespoon icing sugar

FILLING:
500 ml/18 fl oz whipping cream, whipped
225 g/8 oz strawberries, hulled and cut in half
350 g/12 oz raspberries

TO MAKE THE BRANDY CORNETS: dissolve the maple syrup, caster sugar and unsalted butter over a low heat. Leave the mixture to cool, then add the flour, ginger, brandy and lemon juice. Mix well. Grease a large baking sheet and on it place tablespoons of the mixture 10 cm/4 inches apart. (It is advisable to cook only 2 at a time.) Bake on the centre shelf of a preheated 180°C/350°F, Gas Mark 4 oven until the biscuits are golden brown. Lift them off the tray with a spatula and quickly fold them into a cone. Place the cornets on a cake cooler and hold in shape until cold and crisp. Repeat with the rest of the mixture. Immediately place the cornets in an airtight container until serving time.

TO MAKE THE CRÈME ANGLAISE: bring the milk to the boil. Beat the egg yolks and sugar until they are pale and thick. Whisk in the milk. Return the mixture to the saucepan. Cook over a low heat, stirring all the time with a wooden spoon, until the mixture coats the back of the spoon. Add the vanilla essence and blend well. Leave to cool.

TO MAKE THE RASPBERRY PURÉE: place both ingredients in a saucepan. Gradually bring to the boil over the heat and simmer for 5 minutes. Blend to a purée in a blender or food processor, strain and leave to cool.

TO ASSEMBLE AND SERVE THE BRANDY CORNETS: half fill the pastry cornets with whipped cream. Fill them to the top with strawberries and raspberries. Pour some crème anglaise on each dessert plate and arrange a cornet in the centre. Arrange more strawberries and raspberries to look as though they are flowing out of the top of the cornet. Pour a little raspberry purée over the top and serve.

FRUIT FILLINGS

Both brandy cornets and crisp pastry punnets (see page 89) can be served with other berries for a change. Try a mixture of raspberries and redcurrants or blackcurrants, lightly poached in a syrup of vanilla sugar and water and then strained. The juice can be used for fruit salads or to sweeten Fruit Cup (see page 92) instead of raspberry cordial. Peaches or nectarines would make an agreeable fresh alternative, peeled, stoned and sliced very carefully.

GOATS' CHEESE WITH FRESH GARDEN HERBS

SERVES 8

2 goats' cheeses, weighing about
*   225 g/8 oz each*
vinaigrette (see page 28)
fresh herbs such as rosemary, thyme and
*   chives*

ACCOMPANIMENT:
fresh crusty bread

Cut each cheese into 4 pieces and roll the pieces into rounds. Warm them in a preheated 120°C/250°F, Gas Mark ½ oven for 5-10 minutes.

TO SERVE: put the cheese rounds on plates and pour a little vinaigrette around them. Sprinkle the cheese with fresh herbs and serve with crusty bread.

CHEESEBOARD

A selection of hard and soft cheeses such as
*   Brie, Cambozola, Neufchâtel, Boursin,*
*   Petit Suisse, Camembert, Cheddar with*
*   walnuts or herbs, Stilton*
A selection of cheese biscuits such as water
*   biscuits, oatcakes, digestive biscuits*
white or black grapes
butter, cut in small cubes

Remove the cheese from the refrigerator 1 hour before serving. Arrange the cheese with the grapes on a cheese board, with a selection of biscuits. Serve with the butter.

Each serving of Goats' Cheese with Fresh Garden Herbs is an individual work of art that's too good not to eat

FRESH FRUIT PUNCHES

FRESH RASPBERRY FRAPPÉ

SERVES 1

1 tablespoon vodka
1½ tablespoons simple syrup (one part
* sugar to two parts water)*
15 fresh raspberries
crushed ice

TO SERVE:
lemon juice, to taste
slice of lemon

Blend all the ingredients in a blender with the ice. Pour into a tall, iced-tea glass, add a squeeze of lemon juice and decorate the edge of the glass with a slice of lemon.

RUM PUNCH

This drink can be mixed according to taste.

white rum
crushed ice

FRUITS:
pomelos
limes
oranges
pineapple
custard apple

Pour the rum into a large jug or bowl with crushed ice. Add the juice extracted from the citrus fruits. Crush the pineapple flesh and strain the juice into the jug. Strain the custard apple pulp, discard the seeds and add the liquid to the jug. Stir well and serve in stemmed glasses.

LIME AND LEMON DRINK

SERVES 1

½ lemon or 1 lime, freshly squeezed
1½ teaspoons caster sugar
1 egg white
2 dashes Pernod
2 measures whisky
soda water to top up

TO SERVE:
a few slices of lime

Shake the first five ingredients together well with ice. Strain the drink into a tall tumbler and top up with soda water. Decorate with lime slices.

FINISHING TOUCHES

Serve fresh and natural drinks with imaginative touches, decorating with fruit, flowers and herbs. Gather a collection of tall glasses so that you are not constantly refilling, allowing both hosts and guests to enjoy the occasion in a carefree atmosphere. Keep plenty of cubed or crushed ice close at hand, in large ice buckets. Add the rind, as well as slices, of lemons or limes to fruity cocktails for an extra tangy taste.

For special occasions add freshly squeezed orange juice and crushed ice to champagne to create Mimosa; or a little brandy in a goblet with some lime zest and crushed ice, topped up with clear apple juice, to make Apple Topaz.

FRUIT CUP

This drink can be mixed according to taste.

orange juice cordial
orange and lemon juice cordial
raspberry juice cordial
mineral water
crushed ice
angostura bitters (optional)

FRUITS:
sliced limes
sliced yellow peaches
sliced oranges
sliced bananas
passionfruit pulp
sliced lemons
sliced cantaloupe
any summer fruits, such as strawberries

TO DECORATE:
fresh mint

Pour equal parts of each of the cordials into a large jug. Add the prepared fruits and fill the jug with mineral water, crushed ice and a dash of bitters if desired. Mix well and serve in tall glasses or tumblers, decorated with tiny sprigs of mint.

Whatever the weather, whatever the time of day, one of the nicest ways to welcome your guests is with a long, cool and refreshing drink. Choose from a wide range of simple, but effective, decorations; adapt recipes to suit your own taste, and according to which fruits are in season or readily available

GRAPEFRUIT PUNCH

SERVES 1

*¼ measure freshly squeezed grapefruit
  juice
¾ measure white wine
crushed ice*

TO DECORATE:
mint leaves

Combine all the ingredients. Pour the punch into a glass, garnish with mint leaves and serve.

REFRESHING IDEAS

Iced drinks with a fruit base are always appreciated – remember that the less alcohol you use, the more thirst-quenching drinks are. Rum Punch makes best use of tropical produce. The traditional recipe uses lime or lemon juice mixed with rum, sugar and water, but changes may be rung using the juice of a grapefruit, pineapple and/or orange.

For non-alcoholic drinks, blend various fruit juices or cordials and top up with soda or mineral water. Serve from large jugs with a tinkling of ice, sliced seasonal fruit and sprigs of fresh mint.

*Serve Grapefruit Punch in a tall glass
shimmering with ice*

INDEX